Winning Over Worry

Dedication

Dedicated to the One who loved us so much that He gave us the most precious gift of His Son — God our Heavenly Father.

Dedicated to the One who died so that we can really live a life free from worry — Jesus Christ the Son of the True God.

Dedicated to the One who inspired men of God to write the Word of God, through which we can learn, and through whose enabling Power alone such a 'worry-free' life is possible — the Holy Spirit.

Winning Over Worry

God's Solution to Our Problems

George and Helen Jesze

Marshall Pickering

Marshall Morgan and Scott
Marshall Pickering
1 Beggarwood Lane, Basingstoke, Hants RG23 7LP, UK

Copyright © 1988 George and Helen Jesze
First published in 1988 by Marshall Morgan and Scott
Publications Ltd
Part of the Marshall Pickering Holdings Group
A subsidiary of the Zondervan Corporation

ISBN 0 551 01811 9

Text set in Baskerville by Computerset, Heathrow, London
Printed and bound in Great Britain by
Cox & Wyman Ltd, Reading

Contents

Foreword

The need for self-preservation in man causes him to be anxious about his basic needs for food, acceptance, love and many more daily necessities of life. I suppose we all grow up with this concern, but when we meet Jesus Christ personally, how wonderful it is that his power to forgive our sins and restore us also gives us a new outlook on every phase of our lives. God begins to show us through the Word that he truly is our heavenly father and because he is, he will surely take care of us and the needs we have every day. He begins to teach us to have confidence in his Word and his promises.

When I started my first church in a slum area of Pulqwang Dong on the outskirts of Seoul, everyone in the neighbourhood was poor and so was I. Many times I didn't have anything to eat and didn't know when or from where it would come and yet I did not miss many meals. I fasted and prayed many days not because I wanted to but because I had to. I learned to pray about everything and I learned that God was always there. He just wanted me to learn to trust him over everything instead of worrying about everything.

I read in Luke 12:22-31, 'Take no thought for your life, what ye shall eat; neither for the body, what ye shall put on . . . but rather seek ye the Kingdom of God and all these things shall be added unto you.'

I saw the principle here that if I was a child of God and lived in obedience to his desire, which was to seek Him first, then all of my needs would be met. How did

I know this? I put him to the test with the little things first. As I began to pray and seek him, my prayer life expanded. As my prayer life expanded I found that my faith was growing and as faith grew it was not so difficult to understand that where he guides, He also provides. And he did. Not only did he provide my food but my other needs were being met. Before I realised it, I was trusting him for bigger needs until the year we began to build our present sanctuary, I was believing God for $100,000 daily to meet the construction costs. In the early days of my ministry, could I have trusted God for funds to build the present sanctuary? No. God leads us step by step in our personal growth as well as in our faith to trust him for greater and then more greater things. I could not have believed him for 10,000 souls until I had trusted him for 50, then 100, and then 1,000. Nowadays, I am still learning there is no limit to God's ability to perform miracles that would stagger the average person but he is looking for men and women whom he can trust to trust him instead of worrying. We must trust him for the little things then go on to trust him for the larger things which he, himself has planted in our hearts to trust him for.

You can be a winner over your personal worries if you start to trust God for the little issues, one at a time before tackling the larger ones. It doesn't matter if your problems centre in your family, your business, your personal issues of life, your problems which you brought about because of wrong decisions or because of indecisiveness. The secret of winning over worry begins with developing a consistent and disciplined prayer life and a close fellowship and communion with the Holy Spirit because he is the one who will enable us to grow daily in our faith.

Paul Yonggi Cho, Senior Pastor
Yoido Full Gospel Church
Seoul, Korea

Introduction

Each day I have a choice set before me — to worry, to fret, to sink in despair; to look at life's problems, pains and cares; to see no stars only dark clouds of oppression . . . *or* lift my eyes to God in prayer and praise, to worship and adore him, to turn my eyes to *him* and what *he* can do instead of focusing on the circumstances.

This is my choice from day to day. I am free to worry, to let the cares bow me down, to believe that God has forgotten me or — to rise above my problems, to know he is there, to meet each need.

I have the choice to walk the ways of the world or the ways of God; to think the thoughts that just come floating by or to think as God thinks.

I have the choice to worry over the lies of the devil or to rejoice over God's words to me, and see them come to pass in every situation.

I have the choice to be driven to despair, to have my health undermined or completely destroyed through worry, or to cast every care on my Saviour.

I have the choice to 'pray and not to faint', like the poor widow who would not give in to her hopeless situation, but conquered the unjust judge by her perseverance.

I have the choice — *you* have the choice.

Although it is written in the first person to simplify the style, Helen and I have written this book together. It was born after seeing the heartache and devastation caused by worry in people's lives, during our 25 years of ministry, and to pass on some of the lessons which we have discovered together and are still discovering.

We are very thankful to Dr Paul Yonggi Cho for writing the Foreword for this book. In his letter to us he wrote the following: 'The title for your new book *Winning Over Worry* sounds like a very timely and needy title for some of today's Christians who are suffering from stress and concerns of life.'

It is our prayer that this book will bring hope and encouragement; that it will show a way out to all grades of worriers — the occasional or amateur worrier, the professional and the chronic worrier; that it will help to bring many out of the shadows of fear into the sunshine of peace and trust in God.

And that together we might make the right choice of learning to win over worry.

George and Helen Jesze

1

The Start of a Worry-Free Journey

There is in the life of every person, a desire to succeed, to prosper — a discontent of living a life of defeat; a burning passion to win, to rise above mediocrity. We might not know how to win in a certain situation. We may be in the process of being defeated and yet there is that longing, that unshakeable desire to have another go, another attempt, to WIN!

The very word 'winning' expresses effort on the part of a person. To be a 'loser' is easy — just do nothing! Dream along, hoping that things will take a turn for the better, expecting all God's blessings to fall into your lap with no effort or co-operation on your part, and you are on a sure way to losing.

People have won in many areas of life. They have done this in spite of great odds. They have conquered and their determination has held out until victory was theirs. They have won over tragedy and heartache; over handicaps and sickness; over death and the destruction of every hope they had cherished — over insurmountable problems.

The famous author Dale Carnegie once wrote: 'The more I have studied the careers of men of achievement the more deeply I have been convinced that a surprisingly large number of them succeeded because they started out with handicaps that spurred them on to great endeavour and great rewards.' These people did not win *in spite* of handicaps but *because* they had hand-

1

icaps. They had to put in *greater* effort and determination in order to make it in life. If the man in the street has so often been able to win in this way, how much more a Christian who has the help of his almighty God.

Perhaps you have tried to win over worry or in a particular area, but it has not worked. Nothing turned out as you had hoped. Failure is staring you in the face. Nevertheless, it is better to have a go and fail, than not to have tried at all and be left with the tormenting feeling — if only I had tried more. If only . . . Haunting regrets and remorse may want to hold you a prisoner, but you can get up and try again.

An old proverb says: 'Don't cry over spilt milk; get up and catch the cow!' Don't cry over the milk down there in the dirt. Don't try and scrape it up. There is more milk where that came from — from the cow. Even if she is running away, grab your pail and run after her. Catch her and milk her again! There is always a new beginning, a new opportunity, the chance for fresh endeavours. Catch today's cow and avail yourself of her resources instead of bewailing yesterday's cow which is already dead.

It is more important to plan for the victories of tomorrow than to live in the failures or even victories of the past.

Your problem may be a minor one or it may be a matter of life and death. You need to act now! If you are going to survive in this crisis situation you must find God's answer, obtain his wisdom and guidance to help you to win this time. Friends may come and give you advice; they may bring many theories of the best thing for you to do. When Job was in the midst of all his troubles, three of his friends came to 'comfort' him. They sat down opposite him where he was scraping his boils in the ash-pit and stayed there for seven days. Just imagine somebody sitting and staring at you for a whole week, day and night, without saying a word. This is bound to make anyone nervous. When they did eventually speak they were full of blame for Job and angered God by their words.

Finis Jennings Dake in his *Dakes Annotated Reference Bible* makes a very interesting point about Job's friends in his commentary: 'Eliphaz the Temanite argued from the standpoint of *human experience*. Bildad the Shuhite argued from the standpoint of *human tradition* and Zophar the Naamathite argued from the standpoint of *human merit*.' All these standpoints may be important but they will not necessarily solve our problem, as was the case with Job. If you have friends like Job's you don't need any enemies!

You and I do not need empty theories and advice on how to win. Learn to discern what is helpful for *you* and discard the rest. God has promised to give us wisdom in the affairs of life. What type of mother would bring her baby into the world and tell him to feed and clothe himself? What father would send his four year old to build an aeroplane or drive a car? No mother or father in their right mind! The baby is helpless and the four-year-old child does not have the knowledge or ability. They need someone to look after and instruct them; somebody with the capacity and ability to care and someone with the wisdom and experience to build or drive.

If this is true naturally, how much more in a spiritual sense? Faced with the problems and decisions of life we are often as helpless and ignorant as that new-born baby and four-year-old child. We need a Heavenly Father who will care for and direct us. He has nourishment, shelter and instructions for us if we will receive them. But we must see and acknowledge our helplessness and learn to take what he is offering to us. All the time we imagine that our intellect and own strength will put us over, then he will leave us to it.

When the disciples were rowing across the lake against a strong wind, Jesus came walking on the water towards them and, although he saw their struggles, he was going to pass by. He did not automatically stop and help them. Only when they cried out in fear, supposing him to be a ghost, did he get into the ship and comfort them.

The wind ceased immediately; all was peace and tranquillity, and the disciples' eyes were wide with amazement. One minute before they were in the grip of a terrible storm thinking every second would be their last. One minute before these superstitious fishermen had seen a figure come walking — yes, *walking on the water* towards them! Then there was the relief of finding out that it was *Jesus,* his coming into the boat and the storm being stilled. It is no wonder the Bible says the disciples were 'greatly amazed, beyond measure, and wondered'.

It was not until the disciples cried out that Jesus came into the boat. They did not cry for help because of the storm, but for fear that a 'ghost' was walking on the water. But they took notice of Jesus; they acknowledged his presence, his power that was greater than theirs, and this moved Jesus to come and help them. When Peter walked on the water and then began to sink in fear, Jesus did not put out his hand to save him until he cried out for help. Didn't Jesus know that Peter could be sucked under in a moment and drowned? Didn't he know that the disciples were in such difficulties? Of course he knew, but he was in control of the situation and wanted to teach them the lesson of acknowledging their need and acknowledging his presence and power.

Some people cannot understand why God does not intervene more often in the affairs of mankind. They argue, 'why is God not moved at the teeming millions in India and Asia suffering hunger and dying on the pavements; if Jesus healed when he was on the earth why does he not clear all the hospitals of the sick people and heal them all at one stroke? Has he no compassion?' Is he not moved at the horrifying needs around us? Of course God is moved, his heart bleeds

4

for humanity and because he is a sovereign God he can find ways in which individuals can be helped.

However, God's usual method is to wait for men to seek him, to cry out to him, to work together with him, and to cry in *faith*. He waits for his children to pray and intercede for others. The famous Methodist preacher John Wesley once said: 'It seems that God will do nothing of great importance on the earth, except it be through prayer.'

Our help will not come automatically. When the winds of worry and the waves of fear beat upon us, we must cry to the One who is able to help us, and not only *able*, but *longing* to do so.

Ancient Chinese philosophers used to say: 'The journey of a thousand miles begins with a single step.' This is true, and yet I like to think back even further than that first step. Before I take even one step, I must make the decision to *take* that step. When I have made that decision, my mind gives the instruction to my brain, and my brain sends signals along my nerves to the parts of my body which will enable me to take that first step.

The need that is confronting you today may seem like a journey of a thousand miles stretching out endlessly in front of you. You too must make the decision to take that first step to victory. Don't worry about covering the whole distance before you reach your answer, just make your decision and take one step, then another, then another. Don't look back. Keep going on. You are learning to win, to win over worry, to win in the strength and power of Jesus! If you fall, well, jump up straight away. You're not a failure, just a learner!

To get to the top of a ladder, we start at the bottom, then one rung at a time, we climb steadily to the top. A few years ago I climbed the Säntis (2504 metres or 7512 feet) in Switzerland. On the lower parts of the mountain were several tourists enjoying the scenery, eating their packed lunches. There were a few others who, like me, had decided to climb the mountain. Soon the picnicking tourists were left behind and the way became more difficult. It was tougher going. My Swiss guide, an elderly Christian with a wind-browned, wrinkled face and a tough, gnarled figure trudged steadily onwards. He had been doing this all his life; it was second nature to him. The big mountaineering boots on his feet were planted firmly but easily on the path, one after the other, crunching on the stones.

I looked back and suddenly saw that we were alone. The climbing tourists had turned back. The higher we got the less company we had. It was soon easy to see who had really decided to climb that mountain to the top, and those who were fascinated with the idea of climbing but had not made the *decision* to climb and to stick it out.

When we make our decision to live a life of trust instead of worry, and start upon our worry-free journey, that decision must be kept firm within our hearts. 'If the going gets tough, the tough get going' is often said, and this journey will have easy and difficult stages. We have the choice to travel a short distance then turn back, or to go the whole way; the choice of turning back to the lowlands where the fog of confusion and worry dulls and inhibits us, or climbing where the air is pure and where, with the eye of faith, we can see new, marvellous landscapes and vistas stretched out before us.

Don't hang back and say you will never make it. You *too* can win over worry.

A child learning to walk often falls down, but he doesn't lie there for two weeks. If he scrapes his knees, knocks his chin on a chair and then falls flat on his back, he may scream for Mum to comfort him, but he will soon be up and off again. Something within him, the longing to walk on his own two legs drives him to have another go. He wants to learn to walk like Mum and Dad!

Sometimes when we see others who live a worry-free life even in the midst of great pressures, we forget that no-one was born that way. Just like learning to walk, these people also had to learn to overcome worry. They may have fallen many times, but they got up and had another go.

Make your decision today to get up and try again. Cry out to Jesus Christ for his help and begin to take your first step on 'the journey of a thousand miles'.

2

The Sin of Worry or Goliath and his Brothers

A preacher once said: 'I haven't been tempted in many areas, but my greatest temptation was to worry.' At first sight, this may seem a strange statement, for when we talk of temptation, we think of being tempted to sin. But is *worry* a sin? The majority of Christians would say 'No', but let us examine it more closely.

When we worry, we are believing that our problem is unsolvable, that we do not know what to do, that no-one can help us. Our minds are tormented by fear and our problems seem to fill our horizon, blotting out everything else. They greet us when we wake in the morning, bear down upon us through the day and insist on going to bed with us at night.

We take our problem and turn it over and over in our mind. Just like a snowball being rolled downhill, our problem increases in size the more we keep it mentally moving. Not only does it get larger, but it develops and becomes more complicated. The more we worry, the less capable our minds are of looking at our need rationally or spiritually. Our minds become clogged and littered by the debris of anxiety and hinder us going forward on our road.

The solution to our problem may be a very simple one, but because we have given in to worry, we have become confused and disorientated.

A man who has lost his way in a blizzard may have the impression that he is miles from his house, but he could be standing right by the gate-post. His destination is so near yet it might as well be 20 miles away because he feels so forlorn and lost. He has lost sight of the way, he has lost his bearings. Instead of walking in the direction he should be going, he walks unknowingly in a circle, coming back to the place he started from, having made little or no progress on his journey.

Satan seeks to cause us to walk in a haze of problems and worry, our vision clouded, ineffective and defeated, going round in circles and never getting anywhere.

All these symptoms of worry are the result or the growth of the root of fear. The Bible tells us plainly *not* to fear. God commanded Joshua to be strong and very courageous, not to fear or even to be dismayed. 'Dismayed' is another word for being anxious or worried. Being 'dismayed' will lead us into fear.

Jesus often said, 'Fear not' or 'Be not afraid'. He said it to the disciples, to the woman with the issue of blood trembling in the road at his feet, and to many others. He did not say it might be 'nice' if they weren't afraid, it might be a 'good thing'. No, he *commanded* them to lay aside or cast away their fear and worry and look to him in their need.

If we are commanded so many times in the Bible not to fear, (366 times — once for every day of the year, even leap-year!) then if we do fear and are anxious we are disobeying God's command. Looked at in this light, we can see that worry *is* a sin.

Faith and fear are opposite poles which attract us in opposite directions. Faith, which springs up through believing God's Word, will act as a 'currency' to obtain the blessings of God upon our life and solve our problems. Fear comes as a result of meditating on the lies of the devil and, like a bee to a honey-pot, will attract defeat, sickness and everything negative into your life. That is why God hates fear and *commands* us not to be anxious and afraid. He does not want us to be des-

9

troyed but to experience his bounty as a loving Father.

It is not a sin to be bombarded by fear. Every Christian has to fight these attacks of the devil. It becomes wrong and a sin when we entertain and dwell on these thoughts which are trying to overwhelm us.

Many Christians who would not dream of committing the sins of adultery or murder, constantly commit the sin of worry! Sin *is* sin, in God's eyes, and we must learn to see it as he sees it. John Wesley, the founder of Methodism, once said: 'I could no more worry than I could curse or swear.'

Worry is not something harmless, something to excuse by saying that everybody does it, to laugh or shrug off as though we could not help ourselves. The problem of chronic worrying is like a giant which, whether we realise it or not, is out to defeat and destroy us.

Have you ever had an unpleasant next-door neighbour? Things go from bad to worse and he becomes positively aggressive, but if he keeps on his side of the fence, you may be able to put up with him. The trouble starts if he wants to move in with you and live in *your house*, and let his dog bury bones in *your* flowerbeds! Then you realise you have been too tolerant. You have let things go too far.

Just imagine having *Worry* as your neighbour! First of all he was a small baby, then a child, and nobody took much notice of him. But you tolerated him so long, fed him on such a good diet of juicy doubts and foolish fears that he has grown up into a giant. No longer does he keep himself to himself, but is constantly knocking at your door, popping in whenever you accidentally leave it open, and has already arranged some of his furniture in your living-room!

Worse than that, he's brought his four brothers — Fear, Depression, Sickness and Defeat — and they are camping on the front lawn just waiting for a chance to move in and take over. Every time you look out of the window one of the brothers rears his ugly head and leers threateningly.

When you tiptoe out of your front-door, hoping to miss the ghastly bunch, up pops Giant Worry or one of his brothers, ready to waylay you. They are always alert, never seem to sleep and are confident of victory. They have their eyes on your house and know that unless you start asserting your rights and throw them out, one of these fine days — sooner or later — they will have you where they want you. You are no longer master of your own premises, you live in fear and trembling with these enemies breathing down your neck. One would think that *Worry and Co* owned your property and *you* were the one trying to gain a foothold in *their* domain!

There is only one thing to do. Turn them off your grounds, with *all* their belongings, don't leave any of their garbage hanging around. Mend that gap in the fence where Worry has been sneaking through. If he doesn't get any of your titbits, he'll soon be looking for someone else to feed him and will find a new place to live.

Chop up Worry's furniture, throw it out of your living-room. It is such gloomy, hard, ugly stuff, oozing anxiety from every joint until the floor underneath is rotting and giving way. Have a grand spring-cleaning spree! When Worry's brothers are off your lawn, you can open your windows again and let in plenty of sunlight and fresh air. Don't let *anyone* put you off doing this saying it is a lot of fuss about nothing.

You dare not tolerate the worry-habit and look upon something so dangerous as harmless and not worth bothering about. Doctors repeatedly tell us that stress and anxiety can cause heart attacks, stomach ulcers and many diseases. Our hospitals are crowded with people who have psychosomatic (stress-related) diseases, and many patients in mental institutions are people whose problems started simply by worrying.

The chronic worrier is like a person looking at the

warning on a cigarette packet: 'Danger: Government health warning: These cigarettes can seriously damage your health.' More than 30,000 people die each year in the UK fron lung cancer. The smoker knows he is in danger of getting lung cancer, and yet he continues his deadly habit. Even the people around him can contract these same diseases although they are not smoking but only passively inhaling his smoke!

A Mr Smith was travelling from London to New York. His booking was late and the only available seat was in the smokers' section. Being a non-smoker, he took out some chewing gum and popped a piece into his mouth. After take-off the smokers got out their cigarettes and lit up. Soon the man next to him was blowing out clouds of smoke, and Mr Smith became increasingly agitated.

After about ten minutes, Mr Smith took out his chewing gum and handed it to his neighbour saying: 'Would you like to have a chew?' The man was horrified and spluttered indignantly through his moustache something about 'so unhygienic'. 'Well, you see, it's like this,' Mr Smith replied innocently, 'you've been blowing your smoke in my face for ten minutes, so I thought you might like a chew of my gum!'

A smoker affects himself and others, and the worrier, although he may keep his habit to himself at first, will soon begin to affect those around him.

Like smoking, worry is something which we could at first give up or stop doing whenever we wished to do so. But it is possible to pass the point of no return, where we are no longer in control of the situation.

In 1953 when the Russians sent up their first Sputnik, a lady in Nottingham began to worry that the Sputnik would come down and fall on her head. Laughable though it sounds, this worry and fear turned into such an obsession that she was eventually taken into a mental hospital, and given electric shock treatment.

So — get rid of the Goliath of Worry before he gets rid of *you!* Repent of the sin of worry and begin to live a life of trust instead of fear.

3

Casting all your Care

A farmer was driving along a country road in Switzerland, when he saw an old woman with a heavy rucksack on her back walking ahead of him. He soon caught up with her and stopping his horse and cart, offered her a lift. She allowed herself to be helped up into the cart and soon they were on their way again. After a while, the farmer looked round and cried out: 'Why Grandmother, you've still got your rucksack on your back!' 'Oh,' she said, 'I just wanted to make it easier for the horse!'

What the old woman did not realise was that the horse took the weight of the rucksack anyway, whether it was on her back or on the floor of the cart. The only difference was that *she* still had to bear the weight. The farmer had wanted to help her but she only accepted *part* of his help — the ride.

We, too, are glad when Jesus wants to help us, but often accept only part of his help. We cling onto our backpack of worries and are weighed down with its burden instead of going the *whole* way and putting it onto *his* back. God's shoulders are far stronger than ours. You can ride along in God's cart on the road of life carefree, letting him carry the load.

Some people are not at all pleased when they are reminded that Jesus wants to carry our burdens. They are determined to bear them alone. It is humbling to let someone else do something for us. Our pride and human energy keeps us going for a while but there often comes a point where we cannot carry on. Have you heard anybody say: 'I'll do it even if it kills me,' and the trouble is it often does! That is not the talk of faith and trust. It is mere human effort and pride in our own abilities; a dogged determination to blindly carry on in the way we have been going instead of gladly and humbly accepting the help Jesus offers us. What have you proved if your worry does eventually kill you? Nothing at all except your own ignorance!

You might even have this Scripture verse hanging on your bedroom wall: 'Casting all your care upon him, for he cares for you' (1.Pet.5,7). But if you are not putting this into practise then it won't do you an ounce of good. It is just a beautiful-sounding theory but God's Word is a Book which must be personally put to use. It was never intended just to be read or looked at.

I sometimes say that the greatest distance is not from the earth to the moon, but from the head to the heart. How long does it take for a truth which we know in theory (in our mind) to slip down into our heart (our spirit) where it becomes a reality. You can send a man up to the moon many times in the time it takes for people to grasp or believe a spiritual truth. One lady said to me: 'Brother, it took me 30 years from the head to the heart.' That's pretty slow travelling!

A missionary told the story of a native who came for some medicine for his sick wife. After a few days the man returned saying his wife was no better. The missionary asked: 'Did you give her the medicine according to the instructions?' 'Oh yes, Bwana. On the bottle it said "Shake well" and "three times a day", so I shook my wife well three times every day but she's not getting any better.'

This man thought he was doing right. He was sincere but he was sincerely *wrong*. He had not got the medicine out of the bottle and into his wife where it could effect a cure. We too, often make a great fuss about our Bible but do not get the truths *out* of Scripture and *into* our hearts, which is the only place where they will be able to help us.

This verse also states that we are to cast 'all' of our care and worry. We are not to give Jesus the impossible things while we still drag around the lighter problems. 'All' means *all;* Jesus will do all the worrying or caring for us. This part of the verse is only possible if we do our homework. As long as the worries are our own property and we refuse to release them to Jesus, there is no way Jesus can undertake the worrying and caring for us.

A bishop sat by his fireside deep into the night. The cares of a large parish weighed heavily upon him. There seemed no way out of the present difficult situation and worry and dismay tortured his mind. Suddenly a voice spoke to him: 'Bishop, why don't you let *me* worry for you?' He jumped up and looked round but there was no one in the room. He looked out in the passage, but all was still. There was only *one* person who could have said that. Suddenly he saw his mistake. Putting out the light, he went off to bed and let Jesus worry for him.

It takes us a long time to realise that if *we* worry about a situation, then Jesus has no opportunity to work and bring about the answer to our need. In our worry and anxiety it is as though we are clinging onto his hands and preventing them from being free to work on our behalf.

The bishop learnt the lesson of transferring his care from his own heart to the heart of his Father God, who was the only one who could help anyway.

We once visited a couple who told us of their need. They had tried to help their daughter who was divorced from her husband. They took care of her two young children, who were shocked and emotionally disturbed by all that had happened, while their daughter worked and then entertained men in her flat most evenings. She had once been saved but now wanted to

16

hear nothing of Jesus. The whole situation worsened. This lady told us that she came to the end and said to the Lord: 'I can't carry this burden any longer. My health is finished. Do something to change these circumstances, or let me die.' We could see the effects this problem had had on our friend.

As she was talking it came to me clearly again how the enemy tries to draw us into this net until we are completely hemmed in by our need or problem. Then we can see nothing but our need, only this impossible problem, and the burden weighs us down. How often the devil succeeds in convincing us that our struggling will solve the problem; that when we worry ourselves to a breakdown, when we can no longer eat and sleep, that we shall see the answer. Our problems will not be solved through our attempts to carry the burdens ourselves, but when we are prepared to cast the burdens upon Jesus!

After some months, this lady came to the end of her rope: 'I can't go on any longer!' How long is it before *we* get this far? Perhaps 10, 20, 30 or 40 years? The moment this lady was prepared to cast this burden upon the Lord, then he was able to do something about it. And only then! How often we limit Jesus because we are not prepared to let go of our need and commit it to him. In 1 Peter 5, 6 & 7 we read: 'Humble yourselves therefore under the mighty hand of God, that he may exalt you in due time: Casting all your care upon him; for he careth for you.' In other words: I humble myself, in that I am prepared to bring all my feelings, my mind, my pride, my thinking that I know best, my human knowledge, everything under the Lordship of Jesus and his word. That is real humility — my willingness to cast *everything* on him and to believe that he can undertake the whole thing far better than I can!

It is only when our problems become his problems that Jesus can begin to solve them for us. We have the choice. We can either worry ourselves to death and go under in our difficulties or we can commit our problems to Jesus and praise him for the *miracle* that he is going to do!

In May of 1986 whilst attending a conference a Brother informed me that the Lord had told him that we would be moving. So when in June, Helen rang me — I was ministering in England — saying that we had to move, her phone call did not come as a surprise.

Where should we move to? For nearly a year we looked for something suitable. Time was moving on. We prayed especially that we would solve this problem before I left Germany for ministry in Britain on 23 April 1987. We had been asked to leave by 1 March, but this date had already passed!

Helen was asked to play and be one of the speakers at a women's conference, near Frankfurt. She was going to be away for nearly a week. The problem stood before us like the Red Sea, defying us. We had looked for a place, had an advert in the local newspaper, went to see estate agents, but nothing seemed to work. Every place was unsuitable or too expensive. The pressure was increasing. It was a temptation to run from one estate agent to another, frantically trying to find something. Also time was against us. We could not afford to run around looking for a place to live. The enemy was doing his very best to get us in a panic situation, but I felt that the Lord had a place for us. He would show us where it was.

'Trust in the Lord with all thine heart; and lean not unto thine own understanding.' (Prov.3,5) This is good advice for the making of a miracle! When the pressure is on, then we need to trust the Lord and believe that He will make a way where humanly speaking there is no way. When people asked us if we had found a place to live we replied: 'The Lord has something for us. We shall see it soon.' We spoke this in faith, although we did not see anything. We concentrated on the Lord and praised him for the solution, rather than looking at the hindrances facing us, and cast this burden on him.

One Sunday morning after the service we received a phone call from a Sister who told us about a flat. I rang the owner and he told us that the flat was promised to somebody else already, but we could come and see it.

The whole family tumbled eagerly into the car and the houseowner took us round. There were eight rooms, airy with plenty of light, three toilets, a large bathroom and a separate washroom. The kitchen was large with cupboards from floor to ceiling, a fridge with two freezers, electric stove and a dish-washer. The stairs and hall were carpeted and the rooms needed hardly any decorating.

It was in a large country village, but only five minutes drive to the town. Just over the road a stream rushed and gurgled over the stones and the house was surrounded with trees. After living in a very cold, grey flat in the middle of a town for six years, this place seemed like a palace — and the rent was reasonable. We were told that if these people did not take it we could have it. There was nothing we could do but to hold on and trust that Jesus would do a miracle for us! The waiting time is the worst. But it is in the waiting that our faith, through patience, makes the miracle a reality.

Once the decision was in our favour we waited for a few days before giving the final answer to the landlord. Helen went to the women's conference and a few days later rang me to say that she also felt we should take the flat. What a release. The pressure was gone! In a few weeks we were able to move in.

I especially asked the Lord to give us a flat with an extra room for writing. Jesus gave us our heart's desire and now we have a 'writing-room'. He is *so* concerned about *all* our needs. The 'flat miracle' has encouraged us to trust the Lord for greater miracles in the future.

At a ministers' conference I met a big, hunky, 'baseball-playing type' American preacher. He looked as though he would elbow his way through any crowd and be determined to do his own thing. But as we talked, it seemed that he had learnt another way. Out of the blue, he volunteered: 'Brother, I'm in the no-sweat ministry!' I must have looked very puzzled, for he explained: 'I used to fight through everything with determination and do things *my* way. Now I have learnt to cast my worries on the Lord and let him work it out. Why do I need to sweat and panic? He does it better than I can.' It was good advice.

A person who is drowning often clings onto their rescuer in panic and then they are both in danger of going under. In order to reach the shore safely, he must relax and allow the rescuer to take over. Let's learn to cast our burdens on the Lord and let him worry for us.

4

Too Stupid to Worry!

At a ministers' conference, a group of pastors were discussing their church problems. Each listened with interest and sympathy to the others and compared their problems with those of his own church.

Another man walked by who was pastoring the most difficult church in the area. Knowing this had been a problem church for many years, one of them called out: 'Well Brother, how goes the battle?'

Instead of recounting all the problems he was facing in his church, this pastor smiled and replied: 'Everything is fine, praise the Lord. It couldn't be better.' He walked on, leaving the other pastors open-mouthed. Then one of them said: _'I think he's too stupid to worry!'_

The first pastor had spoken out in faith believing that God had the situation in hand and the answer was on the way. He was aware that the more we speak about our worries, the larger they get.

Sometimes we need to have someone agree with us in prayer, and the Bible tells us to bear one another's burdens. But _then_ we are acting in faith and we shall receive the answer. It was obvious that these pastors were only interested in discussing problems and had not discovered the secret of letting Jesus worry for them.

The pastor who was 'too stupid to worry' later saw God bring reconciliation and revival into his church, to the great surprise of many of his fellow ministers. He was not 'too stupid to worry' — he was too wise!

There are many reasons why we worry but one basic cause is because our relationship to Jesus is not as it should be. Our love for him and the love we have taken into our hearts from him has been too small and weak. Our love is not yet perfected. If it were we would have no fear, and only perfect trust. In 1 John 4,18 we read: 'There is no fear in love; but perfect love casts out fear: because fear has torment. He who fears is not made perfect in love.'

Because of the torments of fear, we begin to worry, and think this will solve our problems. In fact, we are only *deviating* from the solution, not having any direct bearing on the problem itself. It's rather like a bull-fight in Spain.

The bull-fighter or matador confronts the bull in the arena. He takes a large piece of red cloth or his cloak and waves this to attract the animal's attention. The bull becomes angry, charges at the cloth and the matador swiftly steps aside. He repeats this time and time again, confusing and angering the animal.

Soon the matador throws sharp barbs into the bull's neck, every time he comes near. Blood begins to flow and the crowd roars approval. The bull becomes weakened by the loss of blood and pain, and death is inevitable although it may be a slow process. The bull cannot reach round to pull the barbs out, and every time he charges they bite and tear into his flesh.

If the bull really knew who his enemy was he would not charge at the red cloth, but at the matador holding it. The matador uses the bull's ignorance to defeat and eventually kill it. The bull's attention is diverted from the major problem — escaping death — to a minor one — charging at a sheet of cloth!

Like the bull charging at the cloth, we charge at our problems with human energy, fretting and worrying, and each time we let down our spiritual guard — our shield of faith. Just at that moment, the devil has the advantage over us and throws his fiery darts which wound and fester, and can lead to certain death if not dealt with. With every barb, we are weakened and confused but instead of dealing with the enemy who is trying to destroy us, off we go again, charging into worry and care, like the bull at the cloth.

When we worry, we are being diverted from the main issue and using our attention and energy for this wrong purpose. If we could see who our real enemy is (the devil who is trying to destroy us through our problems), then we would overcome the red-herring of worry. We would direct our attention to the root of the problem, and not be riveted on the symptoms which he is waving at us or holding in front of our eyes, in the shape of our needs and problems.

Another trap we often fall into is that we do not worry so much about ourselves as about *others*. We worry about our husband or wife, about the children — how they will turn out — about Grandma's cough, and how long the washing machine will go before breaking down again. We worry what would happen if Father lost his job, whether the government will have enough money to pay the pensions in the year 2010, and a host of other real or imaginary fears.

A lady went to the doctor and after a thorough examination, he said: 'I can't find anything wrong with you.' 'I thought you would say that,' the lady mournfully replied, 'that's what I've been worrying about!'

However, some of the things people worry about are very real. During the time of the riots in Liverpool in 1981 I was on an itinerary in Wales. After a service where I had been preaching about casting our worries on Jesus, a lady walked up to me and said: 'That's right, what you were saying, Brother. I've got over worrying about myself, but I do worry about my son. He's a policeman in Liverpool, just where the riots are. I'm worried he'll be injured or even killed.'

'But it doesn't make it right if you are worrying about *him*,' I replied. 'Worry is still worry, whether you are worrying about yourself or somebody else. You will make yourself ill laying awake at night worrying, and the situation isn't helped. Cast the worry of your son on Jesus. He can take just as good care of him in Liverpool as on the quiet streets of this country town in Wales.'

This lady made the mistake many of us have made. We believe that we are justified in worrying about somebody else, even if not for ourselves. But the principle is the same — Jesus wants to carry the load *for us*. Possibly the devil hoodwinked her into believing that it was only right 'as a mother' to be concerned about her boy in danger. However, 'to be concerned' and to take your need to the Lord believing that he is undertaking is an entirely different thing to being constantly worried.

You may say: 'Well, I can't help worrying and doubting. My mother was just the same, and my grandmother before her, so I suppose I've just been born into a family of worriers. I'll never change, so it's no use me trying.'

Or: 'If my husband were saved or more spiritual, then I wouldn't worry. As it looks at the moment, things seem to be going from bad to worse. I don't know how it's going to end! Mrs Smith prayed for her husband for 20 years before he got saved and mine's worse than hers, so I'll probably never live to see him coming to the Lord. Oh dear! Oh dear!'

How often we try to put the blame for our own shortcoming on someone else. The whole of the human race tends to do it and do you know where we learnt that? Why, from our forefather Adam! God said to Adam: 'What have you done? You should not have eaten the fruit.' Adam replied that it was not his fault, 'it was the woman you gave me to be my wife . . .' Adam was not only blaming *Eve* for his sin but even subtly hinting that *God* was to blame because he had given Eve to him in the first place.

When it was Eve's turn, she said: 'Oh, it wasn't me, it was the serpent!' Unfortunately, the serpent had no one to blame; the root of the problem lay at his door, but the responsibility to resist the temptation of disobedience was Adam's and Eve's. The root of problems in our lives may be because of the working of the enemy but whether we co-operate with him by worrying or with God by trusting him, it is still our responsibility.

We may indeed have been born into a family of worriers and worry is as contagious as measles. Mothers who are over-protective of their children and constantly worrying that something is going to happen to them can cause the children to become tense, unsure of themselves and lead to nervous problems. They have not 'mothered' the children, but have 'smothered' them. It is possible to snap out of the worrying habit, to throw away this damaging family inheritance and come into God's victory. You can step out of the shadows of fear and worry into the sunshine of faith and trust in your Heavenly Father.

Joshua and Caleb had to walk through the wilderness for 40 years, until the rest of their generation died off. Every day they heard the moaners and the grumblers, saw the sin and disobedience of the people, but they kept the candle of faith burning brightly in their hearts. Their goal was to inherit the land of Canaan, regardless of what others might do. Our goal is to live a life pleasing to our God and free from care even in adverse circumstances. Joshua and Caleb reached their goal — we can too!

Become one of those who are *too* wise to worry!

5

The Storms of Life

Every person has storms in his or her life. If we expect
that we will never have any difficulties or crises — just
because we are Christians — then we are deluding
ourselves. There can be storms in the family, in our
marriage; our business or the job; it may be a storm of
sickness hurling itself against us; the winds and waves
of worry and fear beating on our boat and threatening
to engulf us. It may be financial pressures or a bom-
bardment of attacks from the devil against our mind.

These storms usually come suddenly. They don't
send a postcard saying: 'Get ready. I'm coming next
Thursday at 10 a.m.' Like a burglar breaking into a
house when you least expect him, so life's storms break
in upon us.

We can see a storm on television or watch a storm at
sea from the safety of the shore, but to really know
what a storm is like, you must be *in* the storm yourself.

In 1970, Helen, our little boy Paul and I were going
by boat from Denmark to Stavanger, Norway. The
North Sea is unpredictable and on that day it decided
to give us a taste of what a storm is like. It was Septem-
ber and the autumn gales began whipping up the
waves and howling round the boat. The sailors tied
down everything they could, but cups and glasses skid-
ded from side to side and finally crashed from the
tables to the floor.

Soon we were filling up every bag the stewards could
give us, as the boat pitched and tossed. Between the

bouts of sickness, when we dared to raise our heads we saw waves as high as a house breaking against the ship's railing and flooding onto the deck. Just at this moment, the ship's loudspeakers ironically blared out the song: 'Oh what a beautiful morning, Oh what a beautiful day. I've got a wonderful feeling. Everything's going my way.' How thankful we were to eventually set our feet on dry land. *We had been in a storm!*

I once stayed with an architect and his wife. Their home was beautiful; it seemed that all was harmony and prosperity. But after the evening service they opened their hearts and began to tell me of the storm which had burst upon them. They had enormous difficulties in their business and in other areas. As I had to drive on the following morning, I stayed up until about 3 a.m. trying to help them in their need.

In 1987 one of the ships from the Townsend Thoresen Company, the Herald of Free Enterprise, was sunk in a matter of 60 seconds. A human error, which nobody had noticed, caused 190 lives to be lost. At first, as the boat pulled away from the shore everything looked so promising. People were in the best of spirits, many probably returning from their holiday, and tragedy never seemed farther away. But the storm was about to break.

The northern part of Germany is often flooded; miles and miles of countryside and town are under water. When the water has finally subsided, it leaves untold damage in its wake. When a tornado sweeps across a land, devastation and destruction accompany it. The storms which hit us in life also bring devastation. Even when the storm has passed, it leaves its ravages in the faces, minds and bodies of those who have experienced it. The storm may have gone but the effects and emotional turmoil are still there and we need healing. We read about several literal storms in the Bible and it is interesting to note how these storms came.

The prophet Jonah was in a boat in a terrible storm. God had told him to go and preach against the sin in Nineveh. But he was disobedient and took sail on a ship going in the opposite direction, to Tarshish. The Bible says he wanted to 'flee from the presence of the Lord'. He probably had the earlier idea that God was only God in Israel, over a certain geographical area, and that he could escape him by going to Tarshish.

Many people through the centuries have thought that they could run away from God or from a situation. The prodigal son ran away but found that *he* was the one who must change. When we run away, we still carry our sin, our burdens, with us. Like David when he wrote in Psalm 137, 7-12, we discover that God is everywhere — in the air, in the sea, on the land, in the darkness and in the light — he sees us and we cannot escape from his presence.

Jonah discovered this too, for as he was asleep in the hold of the ship, God sent a terrible storm. Jonah confessed to the sailors that the storm had come *through his disobedience* adding that if they threw him into the sea the storm would be stilled.

Jonah probably thought this was his end, but as he was going down with the waves and seaweed closing over his head, a huge fish — which God had prepared for this purpose — swallowed him up! God had not given up on his disobedient prophet and had provided a way of rescue. Down in the belly of the whale Jonah repented and cried to God, and the whale vomited Jonah out on dry land.

This storm had come in Jonah's life because of disobedience on his part. We need to examine the storms in our lives and see if they also have come for this reason. Then we must repent and cry out to God to make a way of escape for us.

It will cost us something to do the Will of God but it will cost us more, if we don't!

The Apostle Paul was in a terrific storm (Acts 27).

He had advised the centurion to wait for better weather before sailing further, for he perceived in his spirit that trouble was ahead. But the centurion believed the master and owner of the ship more than Paul, who was just a prisoner at that time. The storm broke over the ship and continued many days with a sky so dark, that no sun or stars could be seen.

All hope was gone of them surviving and Paul sought God in prayer and fasting. One night, an angel stood by him with the message that the ship, but no lives, would be lost. After two weeks of fighting the storm, the ship was run aground on an island. All the passengers and crew survived.

Paul was in the storm which was not of his own making. He was made to take this journey against his better judgement. Sometimes we are sucked into storms through the mistakes or selfishness of others. Even there, God is watching over us and can bring us through unscathed.

Do you remember the time when the disciples were rowing over the sea, with Jesus asleep on a pillow, and suddenly a great storm arose. The boat soon filled with water and the disciples were filled with fear. They could not understand that Jesus was still asleep and shaking him awake, accused him: 'Master, don't you care that we're all going to drown?'

Jesus got up and I can imagine him standing in the boat looking with contempt at the tossing waters and the raging of the wind. He cried with authority: 'Peace, be still!' And sure enough, the wind ceased and there was a *great calm*.

This storm story also has a lesson for us. Jesus did not say, 'Well boys, my Father has sent this storm upon us and if he wants us to drown, then we'll drown. All things work together for good, you know; after all, the insurance companies tell us that natural catastrophes, such as being struck by lightning, are "acts of God" and if he has sent this, we'll bow to his Will.'

Jesus did not see this storm as a gift from his father, for at the beginning of the story he had told the disciples to go over to the other side of the sea. No, he saw Satan — the Prince of the powers of the air — trying to destroy him and his disciples before their work was finished. He *did* care very much what happened to them. Jesus took authority over this storm and the devil's plan was thwarted.

Satan sends storms in our lives too, but we can resist his working and command the storm to cease, in the Name of Jesus.

Somebody once said: 'It is not the storm which defeats us, it is how we *react* to it.' This is very true. Sometimes we see different people who have encountered similar storms in their lives, yet they react or are affected differently. One of them will bravely weather the storm, while another goes under and cannot take it.

Jesus told the story of two men who both built a house. Mr 'A' had chosen a good foundation for his house — solid rock. He was a hard-working, careful, prudent man. Mr 'B' was the type of fellow who took life very easily. He did not trouble himself too much about the future and laughed as he watched Mr 'A' hacking away at the rock to make a foundation for his house. Why did some people have to make life so complicated? HE would not sweat and toil; his house would be built in a different area, where the soil was easier to work with. It would turn out all right in the end.

Mr 'B' was already living in his house, had given a welcome party for all his friends and was congratulating himself on everything going so smoothly, while Mr 'A' was only just putting up the walls. Then one night, a storm broke over the land. The rain poured down and the rivers rose and overflowed their banks. The wind and waves beat upon the two houses in angry bursts, tearing at them, daring them to stand.

Mr 'A' had finished his building and his family were snug and safe in their strong house. The rock on which their home was built had stood for centuries; nothing could move it. Their home had a good foundation. Suddenly they heard screams and a huge cracking and tearing. They ran to the window and stared in horror.

Mr 'B's house had split right through the middle; timber and furniture were being swept away by the flood and Mr 'B' and his wife were clinging to the remains of the roof. Even as they looked, the rest of the house collapsed and Mr and Mrs 'B' disappeared under the raging waters. Their house had been built upon *sand*.

Jesus had a purpose in telling this story. Some people think he meant us to build upon him — that he is the rock. But that is not what Jesus said at all. There are many people who are saved and building their life upon Jesus, whose houses collapse in the storms of life. Jesus told us clearly what he meant:

'Whosoever hears these sayings of mine *and does them,* I will liken him to a *wise man,* which built his house upon a rock . . . and everyone that hears these sayings of mine and *does them not,* shall be likened unto a foolish man, which built his house upon the sand . . . and it fell: and *great* was the fall of it' (Matth.7,24-27).

We must all choose which we want to be — the wise or the foolish man. What foundation are *you* building upon? The foundation of *rock* which means you obey and do God's Word, or the foundation of sand — disobedience and carelessness. Sooner or later the storm will test the strength of the house we have built.

When the storm rages, it is too late to check your foundations. When the wind is howling and the flood is rising is not the time to begin surveying your building plot! You survey the ground and choose your location *before* you begin to build and you put the utmost care into the stability and construction of your foundation, for this is to hold your house.

If you realise you have not built well, go back and start again! By God's grace, rebuild or support those weak places. Reinforce them. Let the plumbline of integrity make the walls of your house wonderfully straight, so that everything fits together.

Jesus can heal the wounds and scars left by previous storms. It may take time and patience, but you can be stronger in those wounded places than ever before, if you will forgive and submit them to Jesus.

Perhaps the storm of divorce has hit you. Your family and home has been torn apart. Life seems a nightmare and you cannot believe it has happened to you. You feel as if you will never get over the agony, the questions, the rejection, guilt and stigma of being a divorcee. Perhaps you are a mother who has been left with children to bring up and you feel bruised and hopeless, angry and afraid of what tomorrow holds. You are not alone. Jesus is with you.

Jesus does not condemn us, even if we are the guilty party. He says to us: 'Go and sin no more.' He does not overlook sin; he is anxious for us to put things in order as far as we possibly can, but he does not hold the sin against us. He forgives and forgets and wants to make something beautiful out of the shattered pieces the storm has left in its wake.

Storms of rejection, storms of ridicule, storms of confusing circumstances; whatever your storm may be, *your house can stand,* if you will submit every need to Jesus and begin to obey his Word, putting it into action in your life.

When adversity hits you, instead of worrying or just resigning yourself to the situation, examine it, check it out.

Have you brought this storm on yourself?

Has someone else taken you into the storm?

Has Satan deliberately attacked you?

Or has God allowed this experience to teach you new things and to deepen your ministry to others? If that is the case, let him mould you like the potter into the design that he has for you.

Learn the lesson, and *come triumphant through the storm!*

6

No Time for Worry!

Somebody rightly said that most of what they worried about in their life had never come to pass anyway.

That is one of the deceptions of the worry problem, that we do not just worry about past or present situations, but we worry about things that have not even happened — about what *could* or *might* happen. A great deal of our time, energy and creativity is wasted when we use it worrying about things that might happen. Instead of using these priceless treasures to make a positive contribution to the world in which we live and the lives of others, we squander them in useless, negative problem seeking.

Man is not just a piece of cold machinery, made up of different parts with no feelings or the ability to make decisions. He is the most marvellous, complicated creature that God created. He is not even just an animal, but is made in the likeness of God — a spirit-being who lives in a body and has a soul (mind, will and emotions). When God created man he wanted him to live in security, in fellowship with himself and with all other creatures.

When Adam sinned, the peace which he had earlier enjoyed was taken over by unrest. Where assurance and lack of care had given a spring to his step, now anxiety and fear caused him to slink away in shame from the presence of God. Whereas before he had enjoyed God's provision in the Garden of Eden, now he must sweat and toil, hacking out thistles to grow his daily bread.

Jesus Christ came to break this curse and to restore mankind to his former state. By accepting his sacrifice on Calvary and becoming a child of God we can be restored to the same spiritual state that Adam enjoyed before he sinned. The answer lies *only* in Jesus Christ reconciling us with God. St Augustine said: 'O God, Thou has made us for Thyself and our hearts are restless, till they find their rest in Thee.'

But even when we have found our rest in Jesus, and forgiveness of sins, we are still living in a world that is under the curse of sin. The unrest and anxiety in the world will continually press upon us and give us the opportunity of worrying and fretting. This is where we must make our personal choice of 'to worry or not to worry — that is the question'.

It seems that some people are never happier than when they have something to worry about and to chew over in their minds.

Worrying has become such a habit to them, it is their second nature. If yesterday's problems were solved, they would look for something today to worry about. Their mind has grown so used to running along negative lines that they find it very difficult to keep their thoughts under control. They have moved long ago from the *amateur* worrying class; they are now a professional. If gold medals were handed out for worrying, they would win every time!

But where do we express a victorious Christian life if we are seething with unrest and worry? To have peace *with* God is to find forgiveness for our sins through the blood of Jesus Christ and to be born again into God's family. But after this experience we need to seek to maintain the 'peace *of* God' which fills our heart as we walk in trusting obedience to our Father's will.

Some people would have very little to talk about if they stopped worrying. Their vocabulary contains so many words and phrases of fear, worry and negative thinking that if they stopped using these, they would become almost tongue-tied. The words that spring to their mouths first are the ones they have made a habit of using. Jesus said in Matth.12,34: 'Out of the abundance of the heart the mouth speaketh . . .' In other words: Whatever your heart is full of, that is what you will speak most about.

Not only would these people's vocabulary be greatly reduced, but they would also receive far less attention from others. Some people take half-an-hour to answer a simple greeting of 'How are you?' relating all their latest symptoms and problems.

There is the professional 'martyr' who describes his or her latest illness in detail, showing proudly his scars like an ex-war hero! Every operation or difficult birth is glorified and chewed over, to a chorus of 'Oohs' and 'Ahs' and 'You poor dear!' which does the story-teller a world of good. When Mrs Jones comes into the meeting and somebody tells her, 'You're looking so pale tonight,' she laps it up like a cat with a saucer of cream.

Harold Hill (author of *How to live like a King's Kid* and other books) used to put it this way — 'swallowing martyr-pills' and 'having pity-parties'. I have been in some prayer groups where they speak so much about sickness (under the guise of asking for prayer requests) that I have gone home feeling sick myself.

But what a way to spend our days. *What a waste of time this life-style is!*

Begin to speak about the good, the blessings which you enjoy. If everything looks dark and it seems that there is not a single thing you can be glad about, you can still rejoice in Jesus. You can praise him for what he has *done* and for what he *is*. He never changes. Make the same mouth which has poured out worries and fears now speak out words of faith and trust in God. If the situation looks exactly the same at the moment, that does not make any difference. First believe God is working and then you will *see* 'what you have believed' come to pass.

A well-known preacher, Sam Jones, was once riding with the engineer on a train. Looking at the steam gauge he said to the engineer, 'Why, man, you haven't enough steam to take you to Chattanooga!'

'That's true,' replied the engineer, 'but we have enough to start on. If we had enough for the whole trip now it would blow us to kingdom come. As we use what we have, more will be supplied.'

So it is with the Christian life. If we will use the faith or power we have, more will be supplied. This is how we grow and make progress in our spiritual life — in wisdom, faith, power and love. Knowing this the Apostle Paul prayed for the Ephesians that they might 'grow up into him in all things, which is the head, even Christ' (Ephesians 4.15).

We know a little boy who went to visit his grandma. He played happily with his toys but soon it was time to go home. 'Pack up your toys, Johnny,' said Grandma, but the precocious three year old shook his head and piped up: 'I haven't time, Grandma! I've got no time.'

Johnny had probably heard grown-ups say this and realised it was an excuse which they often used. Unfortunately for him, Grandma pressed home her point, knowing that Johnny's problem was not 'time' but obedience.

We are all guilty of saying that we have no time, and sometimes it is true; we feel like a cat chasing its tail and making no headway. We may be overworked and harassed, but nevertheless, it is a fact that we can usually make time — a block, or at least odd minutes for something that we really like. Imagine a young man saying he never has time to see his sweetheart! He would make time, whatever it cost him!

When Helen and I were courting, I was co-pastoring in the east part of Switzerland. I was invited back to England to interpret for several weeks for Haralan Popov.

We were constantly travelling and there was little time for us to see each other. One day I decided I just *had* to see her, and set off the next morning between three and four o'clock from Wales. Helen was just getting up when I arrived at about seven o'clock. Her landlady let me in the back door with a mischievious grin on her face, probably recalling her own days of 'love's young dream'.

We did not have a lot of time together, perhaps two hours, but to me it was worth those five or six hours of travelling because I loved her.

If time is such a precious commodity and we can squeeze in minutes and hours for something we enjoy, then why do we waste such a great deal of it in worrying and fretting? The same hours and years we spend in worrying could be put to far better use.

When our mind is at rest, the whole of our being responds positively, and we have far more energy. If we are anxious and sad, we have little appetite and are listless, irritable and depressed.

Our creativity is blocked and we become mentally unproductive, for when we are worrying, all our concentration and thoughts centre around our problem. Our mind becomes strained, our nerves are taut and tense. To be mentally and spiritually productive we must relax, and be 'listening' for what God will speak or show to us.

Inventors and scientists tell us that they sometimes wrestle for hours with a certain problem but cannot find the solution. When they relax, or immediately on waking up in the morning, the answer they've been looking for, the missing piece in the puzzle, will often flash into their mind.

Helen and I often experience this. It's not at all unusual for one of us to creep into the living-room during the night (or particularly the early morning hours) trying not to awaken the other, and write down sermons or poems, ideas for a book, a song which the

38

Lord has given us.

When our body is relaxed and our mind is at peace, God can speak into our spirit and it surfaces to our mind when we awake. Or when we lie awake in the night — resting, not worrying — these are some of our most fruitful hours, spiritually and mentally.

David the Psalmist wrote: '. . . when I remember you upon my bed, and meditate on you in the night watches, . . .' (Pslam 63,6). Perhaps David received some of the psalms in the night, as he meditated. That is why it is good to have pen and paper handy to jot these ideas down before we forget them. If we do not do it straight away, we cannot usually remember them later on.

Another good idea is to have a cassette player with empty cassettes, ready at hand. During the time when God gave Helen many songs, this was the way she captured them. She sang them out — words and music, and recorded them straight onto a cassette. Later on she was able to write out the music, polish and complete them. If she had waited to write them down first, she would often have forgotten them, for she had received them from God through her spirit, and not worked them out intellectually in her mind.

All of us could be far more creative than we are, if we would unlock the channels through which God's creativity comes to us. When our spirit is weighed down with worry and our mind clouded and paralysed by fear, we are like a car with the engine running, petrol in the tank but never getting anywhere because the brake is on. The potential is there but the achievement is 'nil'.

However, it does not mean that creativity can only come to us when everything is going well and we have no problems. Thousands of beautiful songs, poems and books sprung from deep valleys of trial and sorrows that the writer was going through.

Many of Helen's songs and poems came to her in times of difficulty or loneliness. Throughout our married life she has spent a lot of time alone. I am away a great deal, preaching or interpreting, and she used to find it very hard. She fought the giants of loneliness and depression, of fear and worry, and often fell into self-pity. Then the day came when she realised that this enforced being alone could become something positive if she would allow it. *She made the choice* to reach out to God in a new way; to know him better and hold his hand tighter than ever before.

As she looked *upward* and *outward,* instead of looking inward at her own problems, then the Lord began to give her songs and poems. These were not only a therapy to her but have been used to bless many people in their need. It is God's intention that every valley we pass through we should find the way out ourselves, and also bring many others out with us.

The thing about which you are worrying and fretting can become a means of creativity and ministry, if it moves you to look to God and receive his answer. Make every day *count,* instead of wasting it with worrying.

A young theological student had to write an examination paper on the subject of God and the devil. As he was a committed Christian he had no difficulty writing about the greatness of his God. Time flew by and suddenly the bell rang informing him that he had only five minutes left to round off his subject.

Panic gripped him as he realised that he had not even started writing about the devil. Then with a flash of inspiration he wrote the words: *'No time for the devil!'*

How our life would change if we took this as our motto: 'No time for the devil' or 'No time for worrying'. Our hearts, our attitudes and our words would be changed, if instead of concentrating on the problem we would concentrate on the greatness of our God; if instead of wallowing in the Slough of Despond we spent our time swimming in the stream of the Water of Life.

Jesus said: 'I have come to give you life and that

more abundantly.' Overflowing, energising, creative, healing, exciting life which can be ours in the midst of problems and difficulties. Happiness depends on 'happenings', if everything is going my way. But the joy that *Jesus* gives is ours for the taking, when we learn to snap out of the worry habit.

7

Turning the Tide of Negative Thinking

We are living in an age of increased information. No other generation has had the opportunities which are offered us today for further education and general knowledge of what is happening in the world around us. No longer is our personal world our family, and the town or country where we live. Our world has taken on gigantic proportions. It has stretched and stretched until the worlds and happenings of millions crowd their claims and attention into ours.

Through television, satellite and all the technological advancements available today, terrorist activity, violence, plane-hijackings, earthquakes and the searing horrors of war are projected right into our living rooms. This increased knowledge and the pictures portrayed on the screen bring great mental pressure upon us, although we may not always realise it.

The stage for 'worry-actors' has never been better furnished, and these things create the very atmosphere where worrying is the 'in' thing. This build-up through the media of sensationalism and the glorifying of *bad* news breeds the bacteria of worry and fear at an alarming rate. Watching the late-night news on television can produce sleeplessness, strain and anxiety in sensitive people. I even heard of men having heart attacks in front of the television screen because their favourite team did not win the World Cup!

Our world is programmed to the negative and is not

in a state of getting better, but is in a state of deterioration. Evolution says that Nature is constantly evolving to a higher state, but we need only to place an apple on a dish and leave it for some weeks to see whether the fruit gets better or worse. Worse, of course! The apple rots.

People, too, are normally programmed to the negative wavelength, the worry wavelength. We always expect the worst. When the phone rings (or even more so when a telegram comes) we wonder what bad news is on the way. Who's died now?

If a husband is late home from work his wife imagines he has had an accident. If symptoms appear in our body, before we know where we are our imagination runs away with us. We see ourselves being rushed in an ambulance to hospital, being operated on and perhaps even dying. We can see the open grave, the wreaths of flowers, family and friends standing round, full of grief at the sudden tragedy.

But why do we always expect the *worst?* We have thought negatively and given way to the worry habit for so long that we automatically fall into it again. It is not easy to stand against the tide of negativism which is seeking to sweep us off our feet but *we can do it.*

Where did we get these negative thinking patterns from? We inherited them from our earlier father — the devil. Now that we are *God's* children, comes the task of renewing our minds and thinking, with the Word of God (Eph.4,23).

This was the problem that God had with the Children of Israel. With Moses' help he had brought them out of Egypt, but they brought Egypt out with them! They still thought like the Egyptians. They acted as they would have done in Egypt. Their thought patterns and habits were often the same as if they were still slaves in a heathen land, instead of being God's chosen, covenant people. Even after we are saved, we too, bring many habits and the world's way of thinking with us and it just does not work. Our minds need re-newing.

This negative thinking and fear seeps into our spiritual life, even into our understanding of the Bible, as born-again Christians. Satan can turn the Scriptures to work *against* you instead of *for* you, if you will let him. Let me explain.

God's Word — the Bible — is God's love letter to humanity. He is a God who loves the sinner, but also a God who will one day punish sin. It is important that we get to know our Bible and read the Scriptures in the context, then we will understand that God's wrath and judgement is destined for those who have turned their backs on his Son Jesus Christ and gone their own way.

Yet it is amazing how many Christians are plagued by tormenting thoughts of hell and God's judgement falling on them, because they constantly come up against Scripture verses which speak of these things. People who are troubled in this way are rarely those who are wilfully going into sin and testing God's grace to the limit. They are usually rather sensitive Christians who genuinely want to follow and serve the Lord. Their problem is fear and a misunderstanding of God's ways and character. The devil sees to it that these Scriptures stand out to them and he begins to haunt them night and day with thoughts of judgement.

He misuses the very Word which should bring comfort and guidance to God's children and causes it to work against them. The answer lies in resisting the fears and accusations of the devil — 'steadfast in the faith', for 'there is now therefore, *no condemnation* against them who are in Christ Jesus' (Romans 8,1). If — after we are saved — we do sin, then we can come and ask for forgiveness and go on our way rejoicing that we are forgiven.

In 1965 I interpreted for Haralan Popov, a Bulgarian pastor who had been imprisoned for nearly 14 years by the Communists. There have been and are at

44

this moment many others who have suffered persecution for their faith, in different countries of the world. Several have written books about their experiences and there are missions and organisations which seek exclusively to help the Persecuted Church. It is good for us to know about these things and to pray for those in need.

Yet here too, we see many Christians who have been fed on such a diet of 'persecution' literature that they live under a cloud of worry, fear and depression. They forget that with the suffering comes also God's enabling to drink that cup. He gives the strength when we are *in* the situation.

When Corrie Ten Boom was a little girl, she was worried about something. Her father, trying to help her, said:

'Corrie, lift these two suitcases for me.'

'But Father, they are too heavy. I'm not big enough,' she cried, looking up into his face.

'Yes, that's just it, Corrie. And the thing you are worrying about now is too big for you. Your Heavenly Father knows that and he doesn't expect you to carry this load now. When you're bigger, you will carry the cases easily. And Corrie, when do I go to buy the railway tickets?'

'Why, just before we go on the journey, Father.'

'Exactly. God will give you the strength and courage you need in your hour of trial.'

Corrie never forgot these words and she found that the 'tickets' of support and strength were there, when she was later captured by the Nazis for helping Jews, and sent to Ravensbruck concentration camp.

We do not need a Red Sea miracle until we are on the sea shore. We do not need a Red Sea miracle while eating onions and garlic in Egypt. A Red Sea miracle would not have helped the Israelites then. Only the Passover Lamb and God's protection during the time of the plagues kept them safe. The Red Sea miracle came when it was needed.

We do not need strength to endure persecution and suffering if we are not in that situation. To fret and worry that we would not be able to stand if called to face persecution, only weakens us.

There are situations which we face daily that are just as dangerous and explosive. Subtle traps are placed in our path by the enemy, and we must make choices now in our 'free' Western world which may require every ounce of strength and integrity we possess. It is not only in the time of crisis that our faith is tested, but in the daily run of things — 'where the rubber meets the road' — that we also need strength and courage to go on.

Rev John Osteen, pastor of the great Lakewood Church in Houston, Texas, says that the greatest truth he has ever learned (outside of finding out how to get saved) is: God is smarter than I am. This may seem obvious, yet in our worrying we show that we have not learnt this simple fact. If it had sunk so deep into our hearts that we were absolutely convinced of it, it would become a part of us.

If God is wiser and 'smarter' than we are, then he is well able to bring us through the most impossible situations we face. We would not fret and torture ourselves with worry and anxiety, but would trust him to work out the solution that we need. In childlike faith, we would commit our problems into his capable hands, turning it all over to him.

When worry thoughts come, instead of accepting them, let us shoot them down with the arrows of faith. Do not let us meditate and enlarge upon these things, speaking out our anxieties and allowing ourselves to be sucked under by the devil's quicksands of fear. Let us do all that we can do to help the situation and then expect God to do what we cannot do.

In Philippians 4,6-8 we read: 'Do not fret or have any anxiety about anything, but in every circumstance and in everything by prayer and petition (definite requests) with thanksgiving continue to make your wants known to God. And God's peace (be yours, that tranquil state of a soul assured of its salvation through Christ, and so fearing nothing from God and content with its earthly lot of whatever sort that is, that peace) which transcends all understanding, shall garrison and mount guard over your hearts and minds in Christ Jesus.

'For the rest, brethren, whatever is true, whatever is worthy of reverence and is honourable and seemly, whatever is just, whatever is pure, whatever is lovely and lovable, whatever is kind and winsome and gracious, if there is any virtue and excellence, if there is anything worthy of praise, think on and weigh and take account of these things — fix your minds on them' (Amplified Bible).

If we fulfil this last command of fixing our minds on the good, the pure and beautiful, we shall be in the position to 'not fret or have any anxiety'. If we refuse to worry, then this marvellous peace of God will be ours. Our mind — the battlefield where Satan shoots constantly at us — will be garrisoned and guarded, and worry will have lost its power over us.

8

Stamps and Sparrows

As we grow in the Christian life, our concept and understanding of God changes. This is based upon our experiences with him personally. If I am a new Christian I may have the assurance that he is a God who is able to save and change me. But if I have seen him answer my prayers in a particularly difficult situation, then my understanding and experience of him has deepened and become greater. He has now become to me the God who will help me out of my need.

One of the worries that we often have, is the thought that God cannot be interested in us personally. We feel too insignificant, too unworthy, or think God is so busy with everybody else that our turn will never come. It's rather as if we were standing in a queue, waiting at God's telephone box to phone him and tell him our troubles. Hundreds of people are standing in front of us and it seems we will never get God's attention.

This is often our first concept of God; we limit him to being like us.

Then our concept of God grows and stretches a little and we realise he is not just a God who can contact one person at a time, like two people speaking on the telephone. We begin to visualise him as a master chess player who is not only able to play a game of chess with one person at a time, but who is also able to play several games of chess at once, with different opponents. The master chess player moves to the first board, makes a move, then goes to the next board, makes another move and so on. Yes, we think, perhaps God is able to help several people at the same time.

Then our concept of God grows some more and we imagine him to be like a giant computer dealing with many problems and spitting out answers with unbelievable rapidity. But our understanding of God needs to stretch still further to see him as the *Unlimited One* who is far greater than our natural mind can comprehend.

God's telephone is not in just a few telephone boxes, but we have access all the time to him — each person. In fact, he is more eager to talk to us than we are to talk to him. We can reach out to him in prayer and know that he will never turn us away. This is difficult for us to grasp, when we think of the millions of people in every city, or watch the thousands milling in the international airports of the world as I have sometimes done, and know that each has his or her private world with its joys and sorrows, problems and needs. But God is limitless and can help *each one* who will reach out to him.

You and I are precious to him, in fact, we are the apple of his eye, to be guarded and treasured. Even those of us who feel so ordinary, so uninteresting, lacking in talents and continually comparing ourselves with others, gain new self-worth and begin to blossom out when we begin to see ourselves as God sees us.

One day in India, in 1979, I was sitting in a restaurant when some sparrows flew in the open window, perched on the table and started to help themselves to the food. Immediately Jesus' words in Matth.10,29-31 came to me:

'Are not two sparrows sold for a farthing? And one of them shall not fall on the ground without your Father. But the very hairs of your head are all numbered. Fear ye not therefore, ye are of more value than *many* sparrows.'

Jesus did not say 'peacocks' or some rare beautiful

species but just the common, everyday sparrow is noticed by our Heavenly Father, and precious to him. How much more are you and I precious in his sight!

A few years ago I was at the huge airport in Chicago, USA. I was looking for a post office as I needed to send an urgent letter to Helen, but there were only some automatic stamp machines which did not have any express or special delivery stamps. Wondering what to do, I asked at a bookshop if the assistant could help me.

Suddenly a lady standing behind me said: 'I have a special delivery stamp for you.' There were thousands of people at that airport but God put 'that' lady there *just* at the time I needed her, *and* with this unusual stamp.

Just as somebody once said: 'God shows his greatness by the way he treats us little people.'

Even in the midst of thousands of people, God notices those who are reaching out to him. When Jesus was on his way to Jairus' house with people pressing and thronging about him on every side, one little woman with a desperate need reached out and touched his garment.

Jesus noticed that touch for he said: 'Who touched me?' What — amidst all the clamour and noise, the pushing and shoving of the crowd? The difference was that she touched him with the hand of *faith* and to her Jesus became the personal God who takes time to speak with us, to heal and help us.

In India I saw thousands flocking to shrines and heathen temples; offering sweets, flowers and food to terrible-looking idols. They rang bells, chanted and went through all kinds of religious ceremonies. I was told that India is the land of over 30 million gods — but not one is a *personal* God who loves you and me individually, who has a personal plan for our lives and 'knows the way that we take'. They are dead, lifeless pieces of wood, gold or stone.

The only true God — our God — knows all about us.

He says he has called us by our name. We are not just an object, a thing, not even just a number — impersonal, faceless, unfeeling. At a bank and in a computer list we may just be a number, and the Antichrist's system will one day be a number system, but God's way is relationship — warm and vibrant — that is what his heart is crying out for.

How do you see this God? Is he an eternal being high up, millions of miles away who is nevertheless able to see all that you do and pounce upon your every mistake? Do you imagine that he has an immense list of all your short-comings and sins and can't wait for the Day of Judgement to read them out to you?

Do you find it difficult to please God and experience the daily torment of feeling that you fall short of his standard? Are you worried lest he will or has already cast you off for your failures? Perhaps you are trying to earn your salvation like the members of some sects who constantly perform certain religious rites or duties in an effort to score up good marks for eternity.

Or perhaps the devil takes you through his gallery. As you walk through, looking at the photos on exhibition, you are horrified to see that every one is a picture of your sins and defeats. While you are looking, he is there at your elbow whispering: 'Fancy you forgetting that. You've got no right to call yourself a Christian when you do things like that. God does not love you anymore. And just look at this picture I snapped yesterday — you thought nobody was looking but I was ready with my camera. You can't fool me! And over here in the corner is a real beauty I unearthed out of the cupboard ... Why, even God couldn't forgive something like this. You might as well face it, you're just no good! Why do you keep trying? You might as well come my way; I've just about got you anyway!'

Wherever you find yourself today, Jesus sees you. You are not hidden from him. Jesus has sat where you sit in the problems of life. He is not some great deity who looks down on his creatures as though they were billions of crawling ants, just to be crushed under his feet. He is our 'great High Priest who is touched with the feelings of our infirmities', whose heart overflows with compassion to the needy and who longs to turn our captivity.

He divested himself of his kingship and glory just as a man would take off his jacket and hang it up until he needed it again, then put on the form of a man and became as one of us. He suffered cold, hunger and loneliness. He knew rejection and the deepest of disappointments. He did not allow himself to be deceived or swayed by popularity or praise but knew these would soon turn to betrayal and denial.

He was called a 'Man of Sorrows'— one who was well acquainted with grief. His mental agony in Gethsemane was so intense that the blood vessels in his forehead burst and he sweat blood instead of water. Angels came to strengthen him or he would have died there in the garden before even getting to the cross.

Jesus was not just a human example for us to follow, who then suffered a martyr's death. He was our *substitute* who took our place under the wrath of God and paid the price which we had no way of paying. God raised him from the dead and we can now go free. This is the 'Good News'— that the *Father has already forgiven us*, because of *Jesus*. But we must *accept* his forgiveness and be 'born again' into God's family.

But perhaps that is where your problem lies — you're in the family, but you can't see God as a Father; or your picture of a father is so distorted that you don't know the real meaning of the word.

In these days, the Holy Spirit is bringing about a new consciousness of God as our Father. That was a bone that stuck in the throat of the religious leaders who heard Jesus talk of God as his Father. They could understand a god of justice, of vengeance, someone to be feared and hide away from, someone to be worshipped in fear and trembling — a duty to be performed to appease his wrath and judgement. But when Jesus turned the coin over and showed God's other side, they could not accept it.

Jesus illustrated this lesson to them in the story of the two brothers. The younger son began to dream of a day when he could give up the work in his father's fields and live a life of ease and luxury. He dreamed of far-away places and beautiful women. The dream took possession of him until he finally persuaded his father to give him his share of the inheritance.

The father divided the money between the two brothers and the younger one set off. His dreams became a reality until the gold ran out. Famine hit the land and the only job he could get was mucking out pigs. Hunger gnawed until he was on the point of eating the pigs' swill. As he dipped his hands into the trough, suddenly a picture of 'home' flashed before his eyes. There was father, overseeing the farm; all was plenty and prosperity. The whole family sat at tables loaded with good food; even the servants were abundantly provided for, and he — the youngest son of the house — was about to eat the pigs' swill and was almost dying.

With startling, long overdue insight, he saw what a good father he had had. How patient and loving he was, and a great longing rose up within him to see this father once more. He went back the way he had come, with the picture of the father always spurring him on, until rounding a bend, he caught his first glimpse of 'home', way off in the distance. But it's not only home, there's a tall, well-known figure coming nearer, ever nearer, running to meet him. It is *father*, with a face full of compassion, embracing him and holding him close.

'I don't deserve to be called your son. I've sinned against heaven, and against you. Father . . .' But the father doesn't want to hear any more. It's a hot bath and the best suit and shoes to be brought out for his long-lost son. There's the family ring, which shows you belong, to be slipped on his finger and the house is soon filled with the smell of roast meat, from the calf which they've been fattening up for this very day. The musicians burst into melody, the dancers take the floor and the welcome feast begins!

All this time the oldest brother, who has been working, and coming home tired in the evening, learns that all this fuss is because ne'er-do-well has come home again. That swindler, rogue and playboy is getting all the attention and he — the 'good boy' — is not noticed at all. The father is amazed when he hears that he won't come in, and even goes out to persuade him. At his son's accusations of him being stingy, a slavedriver and hard, the father replies, 'But *all I own belongs to you*. You could have had a party anytime you wanted, but you never even bothered. It's right for us to be glad because your lost brother is found again.'

Both brothers had a different picture of their father. The elder one was like a self-righteous, duty-fulfilling religious person (or even a born-again Christian) who is perhaps trying to impress God by good works and church-going, but his relationship with God is shallow and cold.

He scorns the joy of those who find forgiveness and come out of the dregs of sin, forgetting that it was for those very people that Jesus came. He complains that God doesn't answer his prayers, when many of the things he is asking for are his for the taking — through Calvary.

Which picture of God as Father do *you* have, today? This picture will affect your trust in him and will determine whether you live a life of worrying or assurance. The God who notices when the sparrows fall, is noticing *you today*. .

9

Walking by Faith and not Doubt

Jesus has called us to walk by faith and not by sight. Even to believe in someone whom we have never seen; to pray to an unseen God and to believe that there is a place called Heaven is foolish to the rational-thinking, logical mind. Yet we do all of these things and much more, because we began our Christian life 'by faith'.

We made the discovery and make it constantly that when we believe first, act on God's promise or command to us from his Word, that feelings and experiences follow later. For instance, when we got saved, we believed *first* before we *felt* clean and relieved of our burden of sin. If we had waited to receive this feeling first, we would still be unsaved today. The whole of our Christian life is influenced and made rich by the faith we have in our Lord Jesus.

How is it then that after having begun this life with Jesus by faith, we do not continue to walk through each day with him 'by faith'?

Instead, we take matters into *our* hands and begin to worry how God will bring us out of this problem, pay that bill or find a solution to the overwhelming, insurmountable mountains that we see in our path. We *feel* the pain, the circumstances, and immediately come out of the arena of faith onto the quicksands of doubt, worry and fear. If we would stay in *faith's* arena, with the power of Jesus we would conquer in our battles, and the mountains would become a plain before us.

A little while ago we had the wine scare across the

Continent. It was discovered that anti-freeze had been added to some Austrian wines. Thousands of shops and wine merchants could not sell the wine from this company and other wines also came under suspicion. And a short while later the newspapers were full of another leaked secret — that certain brands of olive oil contained a substance which often triggers off cancer in human beings.

These are exceptions of course, and we do not normally wonder if the products we buy are poisoned. The baker and the milkman bring us bread and milk but we never stop to think that they are not fit for consumption. We don't take them to a laboratory for tests. In the everyday things of life we use 'natural faith'.

We do not test every chair before we dare to sit down or ask to see the driver's licence before we travel in a bus. When we flip on the light switch we *expect* the room to be flooded with light and are surprised if it is not. We take these things as a matter of course. If the light does not come on we check to see if the bulb is still usable or if the fuse has been blown. We check the wires and try to find the reason for the blackout because we are so certain that the normal thing is for that light to come on. In other words, we have faith in the power of electricity.

But if we do not see the answer to our prayers immediately, instead of trying objectively to find out the reason then we begin to worry and fret; sometimes we give up completely, declaring that 'Prayer does not work' or 'God does not answer'. If we had as much faith in our Father and his Word as we do even in natural things, then we would expect an answer, and be surprised if it did not come. We would seek his face and make sure we are fulfilling the conditions for answered prayer before giving way to despair or bitterness.

When I was in Colombo, Sri Lanka, in 1980, a lady

showed me a letter from her son who was studying in London. He was a Christian and had lived a sheltered life at home with his mother. Now he was in another country, at university and away from the stable influences of home life and his church. He wrote that he was finding it hard to believe, as he had done before and said: 'Please pray that the Lord will remove all doubt from me . . .'

At first sight this seemed a very 'spiritual' thing to ask for, but as I thought about it, I saw that this was one of the prayers that God cannot answer. When Peter was walking on the water to go to Jesus he was able to do this impossible thing as long as he kept his eyes on Jesus and walked out on Jesus' word 'Come'. But as soon as he heard the wind and saw the tossing waves, he began to sink.

Peter's natural mind began to question: What am I doing here? Men don't walk on water. This is crazy! Then he began to go under and cried out to Jesus to save him. Jesus put out his hand to help him and as they walked together on the water towards the boat, he said to Peter: 'O man of little faith, why did you doubt me?' (The Way — Living Bible).

What a thing to say to a man who had just done the impossible by walking on water! Surely he should have said: 'Why Peter, you were marvellous. You deserve a gold medal for walking on the water.' But he didn't say that. Instead, Jesus put the responsibility for the doubting on *Peter*.

'Why did *you* doubt? There was no reason to doubt me, Peter. I had told you to come. You started out on my word and then you let your natural thinking take over and fear rushed in, driving out your faith. Why did you doubt?' If Jesus said this to Peter after he had walked on the water, what would he say to *us!*

The same thing applied to the young man from Sri Lanka. When young people go away from home their principles and faith are often tested. This is inevitable at some time or other, but our faith can stand the test if we keep our eyes on Jesus. If this young man had continued to believe God's Word instead of allowing his mind to be filled with atheistic or humanistic teachings which were taught at the university, he would have come through, stronger than before. Even as darkness disappears before light so will doubts fade and disappear when faith burns steady in our heart.

In James 1,6 and 7 we read that when we pray we need to ask in faith and not waver or doubt. 'For he that wavers is like a wave of the sea driven with the wind and tossed. For do not let that man think that he shall receive anything from the Lord.'

This sounds a very hard statement, but James is talking here about doubt in the heart which will prevent us from receiving anything from God. Mark 11,23 tells us that if we do not doubt in our heart when we speak to the mountain, then we shall have whatsoever we have said.

There is a difference between doubting in our head or mind, and doubting in our heart. We may be facing a desperate situation and our head tells us there is *no way* we can come out; our mind says it is impossible. Yet even at such times we can believe in our heart that God has an answer. We don't know how he will do it, but we have a knowing, a certainty within us — in our spirit, our heart — that he will bring us through. So even with doubt in our mind but faith in our heart we can still experience answers to prayer. If we hold steady long enough, the faith will rise out of our heart and into our mind, dispelling even the doubts there.

Another prayer that God cannot answer is: 'Lord, you resist the devil for me. Make him leave me alone.' But God has distinctly told us to submit ourselves to him and 'resist the devil, then he will flee' (James 4,7). We are to do the resisting in the power and authority which God gives us. Jesus conquered Satan at Calvary and *we* are to resist him. He will flee in terror not because of *us* but because of the Jesus who lives within us.

We have some friends here in Germany, who have a Dachshund. He is a friendly little dog and always loves to roll on the carpet and play with the children. But when he gets too mischievous, the master of the house shouts: 'Off to your house!' And with his tail between his legs he waddles off to his little wooden dog-house in the kitchen.

Sometimes the grandchildren of the house try to do the same, but does the dog go to his house? With almost a grin on his face, he slinks through the doorway, waits a minute, and then creeps in again when no one is looking. The dog knows who in the family speaks with *authority*. It is *father* and not the grandchildren.

That's just like the devil. We tell him to get going and leave us alone, but straight after we begin to worry and wonder if he really has gone, and it's then he takes his chance to slip back. He knows whether you are speaking in the authority which Jesus has given you, or if you are just having a go and wondering if it will work or not.

On one occasion, the famous English preacher Smith Wigglesworth often called the 'Apostle of Faith' was staying in the home of a rich gentleman who was very sympathetic to Smith's ministry. As they walked in the beautiful grounds after breakfast one morning, the gentleman said: 'I would give everything I possess to have the peace and the joy I see in your life. Just name *anything* and I would feel it a privilege to do it.'

That morning, Brother Wigglesworth had received a bill and he had no idea where he could get such a large sum of money to pay it. He had been tempted to worry and now came the thought that this gentleman could help him. He had only to mention the sum he needed and would receive it immediately. But after thinking a moment, he replied that God knew his needs and would supply every one of them. He resisted worry and doubt and later, in another way, God provided the money that was needed.

Another story is told of Brother Wigglesworth. He was waiting for a bus when a lady came to stand in the queue. Her little dog trotted up behind her and when she saw him, she said: 'Now darling, go home. There's a good little dog.' But 'darling' only wagged his tail having no intention of going home.

When the bus came in sight, the lady got desperate and stamping her foot, she cried: 'Go home. Now!' The dog scampered off and Wigglesworth shouted out: 'And that's what you've got to do with the devil.' We too, need to send doubt and worry off where they belong, and go forward 'by faith' with our God.

10

Take no Thought, Saying...

In his 'Sermon on the Mount' in Matthew 6,28-33, Jesus draws his hearers' attention to the flowers whom God clothes, and to the birds of the air whom he feeds. As he looked round at the huge crowd of people who had come to hear him, he knew that many of them were poor and needed these very things. They were not hankering after luxuries, but had a daily battle to feed and clothe their families.

Jesus knew their worries and that many did not know which way to turn, and he showed them that he cared. He was not just offering sympathy, he offered them a solution when he said:

'Take no thought, saying: What shall we eat? What shall we drink and with what shall we be clothed? Our Heavenly Father knoweth that you have need of all these things . . .' In other words, Jesus was saying: 'It's not wrong to find ways of getting your needs met; it's not wrong to plan for your family and your future; but don't let your heart be so filled with care that it spills over into words of doubt, worry and fear.' Whatever your heart is full of, will soon show in your conversation. We worry first of all with our minds and when it has taken a greater hold on us, our hearts become full of worry and we begin to speak this out.

Worry which is not entertained and spoken out will soon die stillborn. But worry that is cherished and pampered, never checked and constantly spoken out, will take deep root and bring forth the negative fruits of defeat. Jesus knows *your* needs, the very basic and the more complex, but he says to us: 'Take no thought, *saying . . .*'

When we started our work, the 'Voice of Renewal International' in 1974, it was entirely by faith. We had very little money, no car and three small children. The denomination where I had pastored a few years before could not understand that God was leading us into an itinerant ministry and closed all their church doors to us. They would have been happy if I had accepted the pastorate of a church but could not believe that God was leading us in another way.

This meant that we had to trust God and not a missionary organisation to send in all the finances and things we needed. It is easy to say we are trusting God when we have a good bank balance, many open doors for ministry and encouragement on every side, but when you have none of those things and start from the grass-roots then it is a different matter.

We prayed in food, furniture, our clothes, and many other things. It did not come easily and we had many chances to worry and fret about how God would meet our needs. We were often tested to our limits but we were also able to see our Heavenly Father work miracles.

One day a car drew up in the drive and a business-man we know got out and staggered into the kitchen with a box of groceries. He dumped it down on the table and with tears running down his cheeks took a DM100 note out of his wallet, saying: 'The Lord spoke to me twice to come and bring you something, but I wouldn't listen. I've just been ill in bed for a week and he spoke to me again. Take some food to the Jesze family. They don't have enough to eat. He had to get me on my back before I would obey!'

Another time we had an American girl, Janice, helping us in the home and office. She longed for some peanut-butter but we could not buy any in the German shops. Helen suggested that she pray for some. A few days later, some Americans dropped in and left us some American Army rations with lots of little tins of — peanut butter!

In 1970, before we came to live in Germany, Helen, our little boy Paul and I were travelling for seven months. We held meetings in Switzerland, Germany, Sweden, Norway and Holland. This was also a venture 'in faith' and we trusted the Lord to supply all of our needs. Winter was coming on and Paul (who was three years old at the time) needed warm boots, so we prayed for God to supply some.

We visited a ministers' conference in the north of Germany and lodged with a lady and her son. One day she said: 'Paul needs some boots for the winter. There's just time to get some before the shop closes!' She whisked us off in the car and soon Paul was dancing around in a pair of fur-trimmed boots which he proudly told everybody 'were sent to him by Jesus'!

Our Father clothes the lilies and feeds the birds and knows what we need. Nevertheless, we must do our part by believing that he is caring for us and not annul the effects of our prayers by saying 'How will we get through this need?' or 'They're laying people off. I'm sure to be one of those made redundant . . .' and similar remarks of unbelief.

When the Children of Israel were taking Jericho, Joshua commanded them to be absolutely silent as they walked around the walled city. Not a word was to be spoken by anyone until the day when Joshua would command them to shout the shout of victory.

Have you ever wondered why he commanded them not to speak? It was not for the purposes of secrecy, so that the people in Jericho would not know they were there. No, the Jericho-ites were well aware of what was going on and were shaking in their shoes.

But Joshua knew the murmuring and disobedience of the Children of Israel and laid this discipline of silence upon them so that there would be no unbelief being spoken out. No one could influence another by questioning Joshua's command of walking round the city every day; even if they thought it a stupid thing to do, they still had to do it. They were unable to 'take thought, saying . . .' and God gave them a mighty victory.

When we first moved down to southern Germany, we moved to a house, whereas before we had lived in a small flat in Frankfurt. This meant we needed more furniture and household equipment. The children's clothes were in cardboard boxes; and there were many things we needed. Since we were trusting the Lord to bring these things and did not have any money to buy, we walked through the half-empty rooms praising God for the furniture, carpets and curtains he was going to send to fill them.

We did this for several months and one day received a telephone call from a pastor. A lady had died in their church. Could we use any furniture and household things? We were free to take anything we wished. Praise the Lord! That was the first furniture breakthrough. Then the Lord sent things we needed through other people. I don't know what the neighbours thought as they saw carpets, settees and all kinds of other objects arriving on the top of cars, at intervals, to the Jeszes' house.

Once when we arrived back from England after the summer holidays, we found new curtains in the living-room, a new bedspread on our bed and a new tea service set out, all gifts from some dear friends. Our heavenly Father knows what we need, and although we are often tested, he will care and provide for us.

I remember travelling to north Germany to preach, having hardly any money in my pocket. After buying petrol and a meal, it was all gone and I realised that if the Lord did not do a miracle, I would not be able to get home again. Satan was there as usual, telling me

64

that nobody in their right mind goes on a journey without any money, and that 'living by faith' was the craziest thing to do, anyway. As I watched the needle on the petrol gauge going back, it was a great temptation to worry.

I visited some friends on the way back, and they came out to the pavement to wave me off. My heart sank, for I had wondered if perhaps here, the Lord would lay it on somebody's heart to give me an offering. But that had not been the case. Miles of autobahn stretched between me and home, and I could see myself parked at the side somewhere, with no petrol, no money and the police driving up to see what was happening.

I got in the car, the engine was running and I was just going to drive off, when one of the men sprang forward and pressed some money through the window. Then another man followed with DM10 — and a bag of tomatoes. The Lord had given me enough money to get me home.

Somebody said: 'A testimony is what is left after the test'. We all love to hear and give testimonies of victory, but the 'test' is the difficult part. That is hard enough, but sometimes harder is resisting the temptation to speak out our thoughts of worry, to 'take no thought, saying'.

There was the case of the oil bill for £250. It was just one of many bills and things were so difficult financially, it seemed as if God had forgotten us. I was in bed with a heavy cold and had just come back from several days' meetings which involved a lot of travelling. The gifts I had received for preaching hardly covered the petrol expenses, let alone pay for anything else. Helen went through all the pockets in our clothes, drawers and any odd corners where money might be hiding, and we were thrilled to find enough to buy something for tea.

We had managed to scrape the money together to

pay the oil bill that morning, but it was really a case of 'robbing Peter to pay Paul', for now other necessary things would have to wait.

That day some Christian friends dropped by and casually asked, 'Have you paid your oil bill?' When we replied that we had, they were surprised, saying the Lord had told them to help us. It was a great temptation to say we could use the money so urgently elsewhere, but we felt God was testing our integrity and they had specifically said 'for the oil bill' so we said nothing. Perhaps they were a little late in obeying God, or perhaps we should have told of our present need. We never knew.

But in each of these tests we were learning to throw the care on our Father, and one day he gave us a great surprise concerning the oil. The engineer had been doing a little repair job on the furnace, and asked when we had received our last delivery of oil. We told him and he declared it was impossible, for there was so much oil still in the tank. The heating had been on all the time, but the level of oil had not gone down! We showed the engineer the invoice and he just shook his head; we could only imagine that *God had multiplied the oil for us!*

Whatever the needs facing you today, take fresh courage and begin to praise your Father for the victories he has in store for *you*. He is still 'Jehovah-jireh' — the 'God who provides' — and 'El-Shaddai' — the 'God of more than enough'.

11

This is the Day

Each new day is a gift from God. Each new day is a brand-new unit of time which has never been before. It is not just *a* day, an ordinary day, a dull day, a day of defeat. It is not just one of the many days in that year but it is **the day**, D-Day, delightful day, a dynamic day, deliverance day, destiny day. 'The day which the Lord has made.'

Each day of our life is special. No other day in the past or the future will be quite like 'today'. This day was designed and created by God for us, as his special gift.

We might differ from other people, our culture, finances, upbringing, but we all have 24 hours a day. God has entrusted us with these precious days, these 1,440 minutes, these 86,400 seconds. No matter what our position in life, we all have these 86,400 seconds every day.

When I see so many wasting their time, 'killing time', not knowing what to do with their leisure time, I feel God should not have given them 24 hours a day, maybe 10 or 15 hours would have been enough. If I were God I would not have been so generous in giving them so much time. I sometimes wish I could have some of their time and invest it for the Lord.

Here is another way of saying it: 'These are the *24 hours* that the Lord has made for me. These are brand new minutes.' I was in a meeting in north Germany and the Lord gave the following word. (It was at the beginning of a new year.) The Lord said that he gave us, as individuals and also as a church, a new book, with many pages. These pages are empty, clean as the untrodden snow. What we are going to write on these pages is left to us. Will it be victories or defeats? The Lord wants to help us to make each day a day of victory. But we determine what is going to be written. If we co-operate with Jesus, then our year book will contain pages of victory. If we do *not* work with him we will write pages of *defeat*.

Also this word said that we should get a large book, not a mini-book. The larger the book, the more we can write in it. Also the Lord stressed that he is not only the God of the red-letter days, special days, Sundays or times when we have special meetings, but that he is also the God of the 'Everyday', the normal day, the working day. He wants to help us every day.

As I meditated upon these words I realised that the Lord is placing the responsibility of a day, a year, our whole life, on us. The Lord wants to do his part, but we must be willing to do ours.

I heard a saying during one of my trips to the USA: 'This is the first day of the rest of your life!' How true. How we treat this first day will determine how our future days will develop. No wonder Rudyard Kipling wrote in his poem 'If':

> If you can fill the unforgiving minute
> With sixty seconds worth of distance run.
> Yours is the earth and everything that's in it,
> And what is more, you'll be a man, my son!

This *is* the day, not this *was* the day. We have no influence on the past. It is gone. Yesterday had its chance. Tomorrow will still get its opportunities; the only time in which we can live is *now*.

How shall we start this day, this special gift from God? We have a choice how to do this. We can lay in bed thinking what a terrible day it is going to be. My wife is sure to be fussy and irritable again; the children are getting rebellious and won't listen to me, and then there are all the problems waiting for me at the office!

Worry grips me and depression hovers over me like a dark cloud. Anxiety causes my stomach to tense into knots and a feeling of hopelessness and not being able to cope paralyses my thinking.

I don't feel like getting up. The only sensible thing to do is turn over and go to sleep again. I'm not out of bed yet, but I have already defeated myself. The whole day seems messed up, I did not get enough sleep, the weather is abominable, I don't feel well, and self-pity creeps into bed and cuddles up to me. It seems no one understands or loves me.

Depression is no longer hovering like a cloud above me but is covering me like a blanket, weighing me down. I have forgotten that it is a *special* day; even though it may be an ordinary, working day it is special because God has entrusted this day to me and is watching to see what I will make of it.

But there is *another* way of facing the day. This verse in Psalm 118,24 tells us the secret: 'This is the day which the Lord has made; we will rejoice and be glad in it.' To make this a day of victory and not a day of defeat, I must 'rejoice'.

What, first thing in the morning? When I'm feeling like this? Yes, rejoice that whatever Satan might try to throw at me in this day, Jesus is greater. Rejoice that *he* will put me over. Rejoice that Jesus and I together can put the enemy to flight. Rejoice before I feel like it. Did you notice it said *first* that we are to rejoice? Then afterwards comes the 'being glad'. Even if praise is a sacrifice, offer it up to our Father and see him make this a special day. He has surprises in store, unheard-of answers to problems and peace and joy waiting for those who will claim them as their own.

I am so glad that the Lord gives us a new start — a new day. Our life is composed of days. Just because *one* of our days has been a disaster, it does not mean that another day must be the same. Each day is a *new* day.

We can live each day at a time.

We leave the yesterdays with all of our defeats, disappointments and despair and we close the door to yesterday with the key of today. We cut off our yesterdays, and bury them with the spade of today. I must not allow my yesterdays to stop me from concentrating on today.

Paul writes in Philippians 3,13: '. . . forgetting those things which are behind, and reaching forth unto those things which are before.'

Jesus says in Matthew 6,34:'Take no thought for the morrow: for the morrow shall take thought for the things of itself.'

In other words, do not worry about tomorrow for tomorrow shall worry for itself. Every day is a separate unit and we must treat it as such.

Yesterday is dead, today is alive, tomorrow will be alive. We can learn from yesterday — from its mistakes and victories. We must give our todays an equal chance to live. Yesterday has had its opportunities, tomorrow has not yet been born.

If God is the Creator of our day surely he will help us to be creative and productive in our work; he will bless the work of our hands, as we believe it, and walk with him.

And who knows, this day which may seem such a very ordinary, working day with no great promise, may turn out to be a wonderful, special day. It could be that in this day will come that answer to prayer you have been waiting for so long. An unexpected phone call or piece of news can flood your life with sunshine. It may be today that your 'prodigal son' will come home.

Mary, when she got up that morning, had not the slightest idea that the angel Gabriel was winging his way to earth to bring her the news that she was chosen to be the mother of the great Messiah.

Joseph in prison, having almost given up hope of

coming out, felt betrayed and forgotten. Then suddenly there was a clanging of doors, a pounding of feet and voices shouting: 'Where's Joseph? Joseph, Pharaoh has sent for you. Hurry, man. Get ready!'

He was whisked from the dungeon to the palace, into the presence of the ruler of the greatest dynasty of that day — Pharaoh, King of Egypt. In a matter of hours, the picture had changed and a prisoner became the Prime Minister! A day — *a special day*. The ordinary becomes the *extraordinary*.

Then there are days when something happens or we meet a person, and it does not seem of any great importance. But these very happenings sometimes change the whole course of our life.

Or on looking back, we realise that was a red-letter day and we did not recognise it at the time. Let us learn to be sensitive to the whispers of the Holy Spirit that we may learn what is important in our days, and take special notice of these things.

God is always dropping flowers along our path, little bits of encouragement here, an answer to prayer there, but we are so often so busy or discontented, seeking for greater things, that we miss these tokens of his goodness. We often worry and fret as to why God has not answered, and he is often trying to tell us: 'I've heard you and I am answering you. Can't you see I've got the wheels rolling? My angels are getting everything prepared. The answer's on its way; just a little patience and it'll burst upon you.'

Let us accept each of our days with open arms, as an opportunity to discover the mercies of our God which are new every morning. Step boldly, trustfully into each day, not fearfully or grudgingly. If each new day seems to bring only a continuation of the sorrow, pain or trouble you have been going through, commit it all to Jesus. He not only knows your need but can change situations in breath-taking ways.

Develop an expectant attitude, which is really only

71

another word for 'faith'. The man at the 'Gate Beautiful' of the Temple in Jerusalem thought Peter and John were going to give him some money, for it says '. . . he expected to receive something from them . . .' Somebody said: 'He expected to get alms (arms) but he got legs!' For he was healed by the power of Jesus. It was something far better than he could have imagined. What a marvellous, thrilling, wonderful day for him. *A very special day.*

The majority of our days are not made up of anything as magnificent and earth-shaking as this incident, yet they too, can be days with special touches; the sun breaking through a tangle of leaves; baby's first smile; a lone star which shines down on you as you gaze out into the night and its oppression turns to soft black velvet; the rain stops and you manage to get the washing dry; holding your wife in your arms after that long preaching itinerary . . . little things which to you and me become *great* things. This is *the day* — let's rejoice and make it special!

12

Why me, Lord!

Worry does not only affect adults. Children too, can have worries. In childhood some fears seemed enormous, while years later, when adults, we laughed at our foolishness.

When I was about eight years old and lying in bed one night, I wondered what would happen if the Russians shot God. My little mind grappled with this problem for quite a while. I was getting worried that God would not be able to defend himself. I could not imagine what chaos would take place if ever such a tragedy happened.

Pictures of the war in Poland with its suffering and death all around us filled my mind. Charred bodies hanging from the beams of the house next door where a bomb had exploded, haunted my dreams. Father was away as a soldier; mother and I escaped to the country, but we still dared not disclose our German ancestry. Fear and worry threatened to suffocate me at times and it seemed the war would never end. What if this war engulfed not only the earth but the heavens, too. What if *God himself* should be shot!

Well, fortunately this worry of mine never materialised and the war did finally end. Through a series of miracles (you can read about this in our book *God's Interpreter*) God brought my mother and me to England where we were able to be reunited with my father.

But my worries did not leave me. I could not speak a word of English. What would the children be like in school? Did they hate the Germans for starting the war? In Poland there had been little chance to learn anything and now I was thrown into a class of ten year olds who laughed at my different clothes and homespun stockings, and my attempt to learn the language.

I was shy, sensitive and introspective and through my teenage years as a young man, suffered from an inferiority complex. When I was 14 years old I saw a film by Oral Roberts, 'Venture into Faith', and God called me into full-time ministry. I was sure he had made a mistake! How could I stand in front of people and preach? The very thought made me cringe and want to run away and hide. 'Why choose me, Lord? Why me?'

When I left school I went to work in a coal mine and had a dream of becoming a mining manager, earning a lot of money and doing little for it. But God's call which I had pushed to the back of my mind became insistent. It would not be refused and became stronger than my ambition and fears of the ministry.

In 1960 I set off for the Kenley Bible College to train for two years. It was not easy studying, washing our own clothes by hand and living together with a bunch of students of different races and personalities. Of course, this was just what I needed to rub the corners off, but I did not always appreciate it at the time.

Every Friday evening there was a service and each week two different students had to preach. I dreaded the time when my name would come up on the board. The principal and some of the teachers would be there to 'judge' our sermon and give us their verdict afterwards.

At last the day of my martyrdom arrived. I had prepared a sermon about Gideon and spent about seven hours in the nearby Anglican church praying for God to help me. When I got up to preach and saw all the faces staring expectantly, it seemed as though my mind went blank.

Fear gripped me and instead of preaching the required 30 to 45 minutes, I finished Gideon and went through like an express train from Genesis to Revelation in ten minutes flat! There was a stunned silence as I went back to my seat and the principal had to fill the gap in the programme by giving his testimony.

After the service I trudged up the stairs to the principal's room and knocked nervously on his door.

'Come in! Ah, it's you, George. What have you come to see me about?'

'Well. Well I . . . have come to see you about my sermon tonight.' I was wondering what he would say about my maiden speech at the college.

'Well, *it* wasn't bad. But it was . . . hmm . . . rather short!'

He was tired after a busy day and I was glad to leave him to his rest, in case he would say other things about my preaching. I left his room and walked mechanically down the stairs. It was a great relief to me that this fateful day had at last come to an end. I walked outside just to be alone and to get some fresh air. I was very discouraged and cried out in an agony of frustration: 'O Lord, why did you call *me* into the ministry? Lord I am not as talented as others, I cannot speak as long as many.'

A while later one of the college teachers, Elisha Thompson, when he was also the secretary, said some words to us, which were specially comforting to me: 'I have seen many students come and go. Some were very talented. Preparation of sermons came easily, they could preach long sermons, they were gifted. Alas today, some of them are no longer in the ministry. It came easy and went easy. But if you have to sweat, to pray, to weep, to rely more on the Lord, you will eventually make it.'

I knew I belonged to the latter group. A new ray of hope arose within me: 'Yes, I will make it. I will seek the Lord, even if I have to weep with frustration now. I will stay in the Ministry.'

Let me encourage you, whatever you are doing for the Lord. Do not envy those 'great preachers', those spiritual giants, because they have a greater responsibility. God has given them more talents, so he expects more from them. Be content with whatever talents you have. Use what you have. Invest it for the Lord. At the end of our life God will judge us on what he has entrusted to us. I can look over these 28 years of serving the Lord and truly say that he is not a disappointment. I have seen him deliver me from the giant of fear and inferiority complex, and he can do the same for you. Are you feeling inadequate to fulfil the task which God has called you to do? Are you struggling with the burden of past failure and worrying how you can ever make it in your service for God? Even in our seeming defeats we can gain courage that our Heavenly Father is the God of a new start who never gives up on us.

Losing the battle does not mean we have lost the war.
You may lose a round but still win the championship!

When God called him, Moses made every excuse in the book but God did not give up on him. He gave him Aaron to stand by his side and be his spokesman. But it was to Moses that God spoke face to face, and through Moses, the ex-murderer, that he did mighty signs and wonders.

Jeremiah said he was but a child, but he became one of the major prophets. Gideon threshed wheat round the back of the winepress for fear of the Midianites. The angel said to him: 'Hallo, you mighty man of valour. God is with you.' Gideon replied: 'What me? You must have got it wrong. I am the most insignificant person in my father's house and you can see how full of fear I am.'

But Gideon became God's instrument to free Israel from the Midianites.

Then there was Jacob. His problem was not shyness

and fear at the beginning of the story, it was deception and crafty dealings. He stole his brother Esau's birthright, obtained his father's blessing (which should have been for the firstborn son) by trickery and lies, and then had to run for his life. He ran to the family on his mother's side, and worked for Uncle Laban, tending his goats and sheep.

But Uncle Laban was an even greater deceiver than Jacob. He gave Jacob the wrong daughter for his wife (plain Leah instead of beautiful Rachel), so Jacob had to work 14 years for the two of them. His wages were often a mere pittance in comparison to the hard work, and Laban cheated him constantly.

But God had his hand on Jacob. He had seen that Jacob had a longing in his heart. He had laid more worth on the birthright and the blessing than Esau had done. His way of obtaining these was wrong, yet he was eager and hungry for God.

He had probably heard how Grandfather Abraham had talked with God several times, and God had made a covenant with him. And Jacob was *also* in the covenant, being in the family, and as he was running away from home God appeared to him at Bethel and promised to bless him.

And Jacob *was* blessed. In spite of all Laban's efforts, Jacob's own flocks and servants multiplied until they outnumbered Laban's. Laban became jealous and his face darkened when he looked at his son-in-law.

God spoke to Jacob: 'Return unto the land of your fathers, and to your kindred; I will be with thee.' So Jacob and his retinue of family, servants and livestock headed for Canaan.

Jacob sent a message to his brother Esau that he was coming, but when the answer came back that Esau was coming to meet him with 400 men, 'Jacob was greatly afraid and distressed'.

Jacob's past had caught up with him! He remembered how he had deceived Esau, and was sure that

Esau was coming to kill him.

Immediately he began to scheme and plan how he could get out of this dilemma by separating the people and flocks into two companies. He was possessed with fear and worry and cried out to God to save their lives. He prepared a generous present for Esau and sent it with all the rest of the company over the brook. But the Bible says that *he* was left *alone*, and a 'man' wrestled with Jacob until the dawn. The 'man' or angel said, 'Let me go', but Jacob said:

'I will not let you go, except you bless me. And he said unto him, What is your name? And he said, Jacob. And he said, Your name shall be called no more Jacob, but *Israel:* for as a prince you have power with God and with men, and have prevailed' (Genesis 32,26-28).

Jacob was pleading and wrestling for an answer to his prayers and for God's blessing, but did not realise that he was *already blessed*. The angel said that he had power and influence, and a new name. The old name Jacob — the deceiver — had been replaced by 'Israel' — 'a prince'. God had been working in him and for him, without him realising it.

The angel blessed him and then left, and Jacob rose up a new man. No longer did he slink behind the rest of his retinue. He put his wives and children behind him and he went in front of them to meet Esau.

Instead of Esau coming to kill him, he ran to meet Jacob, and the brothers wept and embraced, reunited after 20 years. All was forgiven and forgotten. Jacob's fears had not been realised.

All too often, our past catches up with us. Old memories, unpleasant memories, ones we would like to leave locked away, buried, gone for ever, suddenly pop up when we least expect them.

Fear grips us and the suffocating feeling of not being able to escape threatens to overwhelm us — *acute worry*. Like Jacob, we often try to work out how to avoid the consequences of our wrongdoing. We scheme and plot and cover up, but this is not the answer.

Jacob's answer lay in this meeting with God, this encounter with a divine mind and a being who was greater than his intellectual ability could comprehend. He saw his helplessness and threw himself on God's mercy and help, realising that falling back into his old methods of scheming would not help him.

How often God has to get us alone, just him and us, nobody else; nobody else to turn to for help or to ask for advice. *Only God and me personally.* It is here that he melts and moulds us, breaks us if necessary, and makes a beautiful vessel out of the cracked, hard clay in his hand — a vessel and life according to *his plan.*

Jacob's answer also lay in the fact that God had already been working in him and for him. 'You have power with God and with men, and have *prevailed.*' He was a *prince*, with authority bestowed on him by God; his sons would later father the 12 tribes of Israel and the Messiah was to be born from one of these.

Our answers too, lie in acknowledging and believing that *God is working in us.* God sees us not just as we are, but as he is going to make us. He sees potential in every man or woman. He knows the struggles we experience and as we look to him he will bring us through victorious.

Shyness and fear can be replaced with courage; being too much concerned about our own feelings can be changed into a loving sensitivity to the needs of others through the working of the Holy Spirit in our lives. Deceit and sin can be washed away; our name can be changed. I no longer say, 'Why me, Lord?' I just praise him that it is so, and revel in the truth of Philippians 1,6: 'Being confident of this very thing, that he which has begun a good work in you will perform it (or: *complete* it) until the day of Jesus Christ . . .'

13

Beating the 'Grasshopper-Complex'

Once I was facing a great problem and there seemed no way out. The more I thought about this problem the greater it grew. Just then, the Lord spoke gently to my spirit, strengthening me through these words: 'Never lose sight of the greatness of your God. Always keep the greatness of your God before your eyes and then your faith will be strong. Do not see the greatness of the enemy, the greatness of your problems, but the greatness of your God.'

How often we forget how great our God is. We sing in the services 'How Great Thou Art', but after the meeting we tell our friends how great our problems are, how great the devil is and about all the impossibilities that we face. It is strange that after the meeting, our God seems to shrink until he is no bigger than we are. We could almost put him in our pocket like a shrunk balloon. In the meeting, he was the Almighty, the Provider, the Solver of all problems, but after the meeting his power to help us ceases.

We are hypnotised by our problems and so we do not see the greatness of our God. God is a jealous God and he does not want us to give more attention to our problems than to him. He wants to be *first* in our lives and not be ejected out of that place by problems.

When Jesus was on earth no problem that confronted him was too great. He was always master of the situation. He never said to anyone: 'I'm sorry I can't help you.' Only the people in Nazareth who were filled with unbelief, and those who were trying to outwit him, or turned deliberately against him — these were the people he could not help. It is often easier for us to believe that Jesus was master of every situation when he was on the earth than to believe that he has our present situation under control. But in Heb.13,8 we read that Jesus Christ is the same, yesterday, today and for ever.

The way many Christians talk it would seem that the devil is getting stronger and stronger, and God is getting weaker and weaker. They see evil increasing on every hand and often quote from the Bible verses such as 'The love of many shall become cold' and 'Fear not, little flock . . .' They see themselves as a little band of sailors clinging to a ship which is just about to go under the waves; or they are trying to 'hold the Gospel fort' with the devil and all his demons over the wall holding them in siege.

Dead and dying, wounded fellow-Christians are all around them and their cause looks as though it is lost. It seems only a matter of time before the devil and the Anti-christ manage to burst open the fortress gates and march in and take over. They are using their last strength to hold the colours flying, but they've lost sight of their captain — the God of Hosts. They have forgotten the *greatness of their God*.

While it is a fact that the devil is winning many rounds in our day, nevertheless, he is not going to win the final battle. Have you ever read the end of the Book? *We win!* God's children win because of their great God. Not only is the power of evil increasing because we are in 'the last days', *but* the power of the Holy Spirit is also being poured out upon the earth in an unprecedented manner. Thousands of people are being saved throughout the earth every single day.

Our God will never be outdone by Satan, but we must have eyes to see these things. It is not always possible to see them with our *physical* eyes, but with our *spiritual* eyes.

The king of Syria sent a troop to Samaria to capture the prophet Elisha. Elisha's servant went out early in the morning and saw the huge army outside the city, and he was filled with fear. But Elisha said: 'Fear not for they who are with us are more than they that be with them.' Then he prayed: 'Lord, open his eyes that he might see.' God opened the young man's spiritual eyes and he saw that the mountain was full of horses and chariots of fire. He saw God's heavenly army which was far greater and more numerous than the army of the King of Syria.

Three years ago, in June, I drove to England by car, expecting to have eight weeks of meetings. Helen and the children were to join me later when the school holidays began: then we would have our normal 'bus-man's holiday' of visiting relatives, friends and ministry. On my arrival in England I found out that, for various reasons, the eight-week itinerary which was being planned for me had not worked out as hoped. On looking at the meagre list of bookings, the enemy said to me: 'That's not much of an itinerary. Here you've come for three months and you won't have any meetings. Where's your money going to come from? God has forgotten you and let you down. What are you going to do now? This is your bread and butter. You know you're not supported by a missionary organisation.'

It was very quiet, only the sound of the waves breaking on the beach could be heard a short distance away. But then I was reminded that as God had kept these waves coming and going through the generations, in constant rhythm, how much greater was his faithfulness to me — his child.

I closed my spiritual ears to the voice of the enemy and began to quote aloud the promises of God. Instead of focusing my attention on the unpaid bills waiting at home, and the family which needed to be provided for, I turned my eyes to Jesus. I was reminded of the editorial I had written in our previous magazine: 'Never lose sight of the greatness of your God.'

How often we sing the chorus, 'It is no secret what God can do . . .' (The German translation says: 'There are no limits to what God can do . . .'). During recent months, the Lord has been speaking to me about this thought. In Psalm 78,41 we read: '. . . they limited the Holy One of Israel from giving them his blessings' (Living Bible translation).

Is it possible that a person can limit God? Yes, the Children of Israel limited the working of God in their lives. The Lord said to Joshua: 'Every place that the sole of your foot shall tread upon, that have I given unto you . . .' (Joshua 1,3). From God's side, the promise was: 'Every place . . .', but the promise could only be fulfilled if Israel was prepared to obey God. The condition to be fulfilled was '. . . that the sole of your foot shall tread upon . . .' — this was the human side. God was prepared to give Israel as much land as they were prepared to tread upon. *Israel set the boundary, as to how far God was able to work.*

Our boundaries or limitations show themselves in problems, in sickness, in financial difficulties, our families, the saving of our loved ones, in our area, our church life, etc.

So often, we limit Jesus by our intellect or the natural mind. We cannot imagine how Jesus can solve our problem, how he can heal our illness. It seems that we are hypnotised by our problem, and caught like a fly in a spider's web — powerless, although it makes frantic attempts to break loose. The spider's web draws tighter and tighter, the fly makes the last struggle and then it is over — dead!

We limit Jesus by doubting his Word. How many Christians believe what the devil tells them, rather than the Word of God. How many are more convinced of the power of their illness, of their problems, rather than believing that *Jesus is stronger* than the sickness and the need. Many cannot believe that their relatives will be saved, because they look only at the outward appearances.

We limit Jesus by our five senses — seeing, hearing, feeling, smelling and tasting. We have a wrong understanding of what the Bible tells us about *faith.* Many people think that if everything they feel, see and experience is in order, *then* they are prepared to *believe.* But *faith is not dependent on our feelings.* Faith does not look at what our eyes can see; it does not let itself be influenced by circumstances, but is based solely upon the Word of God. What we can *see* is very limited. Our *hearing* is very limited, for we can only hear a certain distance. Our *feelings* are very limited. Our *tasting* and *smelling* are also limited, but there are *no limits to the power of Jesus.*

It could be that we are in a certain place or hall and hear nothing, but directly in this hall there is music, conversation and singing going on. How is this possible? There are constant radio and television signals being sent through the ether waves in the atmosphere, but we cannot hear them because we have no receiver — no radio or television set switched on. Faith is our 'receiving-set' which tunes us in to the power of God and brings it into our world or point of need. Because we have based our faith on the promises of God in his Word they become a reality.

We need a Jesus who is greater than our five senses, a Jesus who is greater than our puny mind and understanding.

Moses led the Children of Israel out of the slavery of Egypt and it was God's intention that they should have a beautiful land of their own. He sent 12 men to spy out the land of Canaan and to bring back a report of this land which God had chosen for them. The 12 spies returned after 40 days. Ten of them said it was a marvellous, prosperous land. The bunch of grapes they brought back with them was so large that two men had to carry it between them! 'The land *flows* with milk and honey. BUT — the cities are very large and have walls round them. The people are so tall — we never saw anybody so big and strong. There are even giants there, the sons of Anak. We felt just like grasshoppers in comparison to them, and that's how they saw us, too. Moses, it's impossible for us to take the land! It would have been better for us to die in Egypt, for here the situation is hopeless.'

But the other two, Joshua and Caleb, said: 'Let us go up at once. We are *well able* to take it. Let's go in and possess this marvellous land.'

All 12 spies saw the land, with its positive and negative aspects. They saw the rich vegetation and abundance, and also the walled cities and the giants. What made them give conflicting reports? Why were ten filled with fear and unbelief while Joshua and Caleb were sure they could take the land.

The answer lies in the sentence: '. . . we were in our own sight as grasshoppers, and so we were in their sight (i.e. the giants').'

The ten spies were too busy seeing the greatness of the enemy and the problems, too busy looking at their own small stature and faith.

Joshua and Caleb turned their eyes away from the huge giants, did not even consider their own ability and looked to the greatness of their God. *He* would fight their battles! He was *far greater* than any Amalekite or giant that might raise its ugly head. Canaan was as good as theirs!

But we know the story that Joshua and Caleb were outnumbered, and that this generation of Israelites never set foot in Canaan; their corpses were buried in the wilderness. Only the two who never lost sight of the greatness of their God remained alive and were able to later claim their inheritance in the land.

We too have the choice of seeing only the greatness

of the problem or of turning our eyes on the One who is far greater and has the solution, the victory which we need.

Never compare the size of the problem with your own size or ability.

A small iron bar can lever a large boulder. A small cigarette end can start a huge forest fire. Have you heard the song: 'It only takes a spark to get a fire going . . .' From a minute sperm comes forth the miracle of a new human being. Yes, small, sometimes seemingly insignificant things can have a tremendous effect on a situation. But if you must compare sizes, then compare the size of the problem with the size of your God; then you will get things into correct perspective and see which is really the greatest.

In Eph.2,6 we read that 'God hath raised us up together and made us sit together in heavenly places in Christ Jesus,' right *now,* here on this earth, in the midst of our struggles and problems. Jesus does not look up to difficulties and needs. They do not tower above him and threaten to crush him at any moment. He looks down on *them.* He has them under his feet and has already placed his foot on the neck of his enemies.

To be 'seated with Christ in heavenly places' is a position we take up by faith. We do not take it physically, but spiritually. When we have seen this truth and take up our position with Jesus, then we, with him, look *down* upon the problems, instead of looking *up* to them.

Someone once said: 'If you have a message for Satan, write it on the soles of your feet.' What does this mean? Do you remember the verse in Romans 16.20: 'The God of peace shall bruise Satan under your feet shortly'? That is where he belongs, under our spiritual feet. He and the problems he brings should be looking up at us where we sit together with Christ from where we've got him down in the ring.

On the front of Harold Hill's book *How to be a Winner*

is a huge, clenched fist in a boxing glove. In the background is a picture of the devil on his back, out for the count and seeing stars! Stop comparing yourself with the giant of your problems and see this new picture — your great God causing you to be victorious.

Don't look at yourself as a *grasshopper*. You are God's child, bought with the blood of Jesus. You are somebody to be reckoned with, clothed in spiritual armour and *strong in the Lord,* not a grasshopper to be crushed under the heel of the giant of Worry. Act as though God's Word is true. Through the greatness of your God, turn the situation around, go in and conquer your Jerichos today.

14

Plums in Apple-Strudel

Have you ever eaten apple-strudel? It is a delicious German/Austrian delicacy — a roll of puff-pastry filled with apples, nuts and raisins, to be eaten piping hot. Tempting to the palate but devastating for dieters!

Have you ever tried *baking* an apple-strudel? We know that if a housewife with a good recipe follows it exactly, she will get a good cake or pie. However, if she does not follow the recipe but just puts into the mixture whatever she thinks, then the result could be disastrous.

Let us just say that a lady would like to bake an apple-strudel. From the recipe she reads: apples, raisins, milk, butter, flour, etc. Then she says to herself: 'I wonder what that means — apples? I think plums are much better, especially if I leave the stones in. I'll get even with my family.' And so she takes plums instead of apples, because they are more nourishing. The next thing is flour. 'O,' says the lady, 'I won't put flour in, I don't like it. It's too powdery. Sand is much better.' So she takes sand instead of flour. Instead of baking it the required time, she bakes it for five minutes! She has made this strudel according to her own ideas and not as the book says, because she thinks she knows better. She may call the result apple-strudel, but it certainly will not look and taste like it. It will be impossible to eat.

In India I ate some very good curry. If I brought

back a curry recipe, a lady here in Europe would also be able to make a good curry, if she *followed the recipe*. But if she put in all kinds of other things, then the end product would be far from delicious curry.

What am I trying to say here? Simply this — so many people do the same with the Word of God. They hear the Word preached, but instead of trying to act upon God's recipe *exactly as it is written,* they try to put *their own recipe into practice.* It is no wonder that they then produce apple-strudel with plums!

The Word of God is far more reliable than any recipe book. If we are prepared in the normal, every-day scheme of things to trust what the cookery book says, then we are saying that the person who wrote this book knows all about cookery and baking. *How much more should we also be prepared to take God's Word as truth and the only recipe for our lives.* Oh yes, we say, the recipe is very good, only the acting on and putting into practice of the recipe has not brought the desired results. The Word of God is reliable, but because we are not prepared to take the recipe literally and carry it out, just as it is written, we obtain quite different results, than the Word of God promises us.

We never read in the Bible that we should consult our feelings, hearing, what we see, taste or smell and then use God's recipe. Our five senses are limited and do not give us a clear picture as God sees the situation. Therefore, the Lord is saying to us: Try my recipe and do not rely on your five senses. Use my recipe and you will see how wonderful the results will be.

But, many say, suppose it doesn't work? A housewife can stand for days in her kitchen and ask herself if this recipe is reliable or not. She can turn it over in her mind again and again, and will not come to any conclusion. But if she is prepared to use the recipe as it says, then she will soon see if it works or not. It is exactly the same with God's Word. So many Christians study the Bible and take it to pieces. They put it into the computer of their minds and because the computer does not work properly, they get the wrong answer. Isaiah 1,5: 'The whole head is sick . . .' (speaking of course, of the reasoning of the natural man). Therefore, we read in James 1,22, 'Be ye therefore, doers of the Word and not hearers only, deceiving yourselves.'

If we hear the Word of God and do not obey it or act upon it immediately, then doubts come into our hearts which undermine the authority of God's Word and we talk ourselves out of God's promises. We will never act upon God's Word and we will never receive the results the Bible promises us.

Millions of people today and in years gone by are and have been using God's recipe. Praise the Lord! It works. If human beings can invent good recipes, *how much more is God's recipe able to change our life, our situation, our problems?* And not only to change our problems and situation but also to change *us*.

Friend, why not try to take the Word of God just as it is written, in the coming days. How foolish it would be if a housewife were to say: 'It says in the recipe that I must use flour, but it could be that the person who wrote this means I should take that in a *spiritual* sense, not literally. Perhaps he meant something similar, or perhaps at the time he wrote this there was another kind of flour, which is not available today. In my grandmother's day, there was something like that, but today there isn't such good flour anymore.'

It is exactly the same when people say: *'The Bible's recipe was only good for the early Church. Today we cannot expect the results which they had.'* In other words, they are saying God's recipe is not to be taken *literally* today as they did at that time. Then the Lord healed many people, but this doesn't work anymore. Also in the early Church, Jesus filled people with the power of His Holy Spirit, but not any more. Then, many people were saved, but not today.

But this is not so! God's recipe for our generation has not changed. Nowhere in the Bible do we read that God has a modern recipe for 1988, a substitute for the old one. No, a thousand times, no! *God's recipe is as powerful and workable today* as in the time of Jesus and the early Church. It depends on us. If we are prepared to follow this recipe in every detail, we will obtain the same results as they received.

The closer we follow God's recipe, the closer or more perfect will be the results we obtain. We have the choice — our own recipes, those of our denomination or tradition, or the *original recipe* to obtain the results God wants us to have.

In these days, the Holy Spirit is trying to show us God's recipe in a new way. Everywhere, where people are prepared to use it, they experience that God's recipe is up-to-date and works today.

It is the old principle that what I put into something determines what I will get out. If I put ten pence into a slot machine, I cannot expect to receive goods for £10. It is goods to the value of my payment or reaping what I have sown.

We are all familiar with the picture of the farmer ploughing the land, preparing the soil and sowing his seed. At harvest time we see the crops being brought in, the hay being made and all the richness of the fruits of autumn being stored to feed man and beast.

But have you ever thought what a strange world it would be if a farmer planted potatoes and produced cabbages? How terrible if marrows grew on vines instead of grapes. It would be chaos!

In Genesis 1,11–12 we read that God put the seed of a tree inside that tree or plant, and only that particular kind of tree or plant would be produced from that seed. In other words, he put apple seeds inside apples. He didn't put *cucumber* seeds inside apples. The cucumber seeds were in their proper place — inside cucumbers! What confusion would have resulted if God had not thought so logically.

We are so used to this order of things, it seems impossible to imagine it any other way. Why is it then that we do not expect this same principle to work in our own lives? In Gal. 6,7 we read: 'Be not deceived; God is not mocked: for whatsoever a man soweth, that shall he also reap.'

We understand that sowing the thoughts and acts of sin in our life will bring us a disastrous harvest, but what about all those seeds of worry and fear we have sown through the years? If we are not already reaping their harvest we soon will be. The only crop which will grow without any effort on our part is weeds. Or perhaps you are leaving it all to God, and not realising that *you* have a part to play in the production of a harvest of blessing in your life, like the old farmer in Helen's poem:

THE FARMER

I'd like to have a harvest, the farmer said one day
And so he went and looked at his fields down along
    the way.
Well, you'd better plant some seed, his wife then she
    said.
O no, the Lord will do it all! and off he went to bed.
And so he daily dreamed about a golden harvest fair
And told his friends and neighbours: You'll see it
    standing there.
But he never took the trouble even once to plough
    the land
And he never sowed any seed from his foolish hand.
He said, My God, He is so great, there's nothing He
    can't do,
He's promised seedtime and harvest and I shall see it
    too!
And so the weeks grew into months and the months
    grew into years
But still there was no harvest, no grain, no golden
    ears.

Now before you laugh at this old man who didn't
  sow any seeds
Just ask yourself the question, Haven't you got any
  needs?
And you just sit there wondering why the answer
  doesn't come
And why the Lord doesn't answer you and why the
  thing isn't done.
And why your finances are so low and the problems
  are there still,
And why your family's still unsaved or you're still
  sick and ill.
Have you been sowing the devil's seed of worry, fear
  and doubt
And then expected a harvest of blessing will one day
  come about.
It never did work in the past and it won't work today,
For if you want God's blessings, you must do things
  in God's way.
So throw away the devil's seed and use the Lord's
  instead,
Plant it deep in your spirit. It will bring forth, He's
  said.
With faith and patience you will see the promises
  come true.
God's law of sowing and reaping, and it will work for
  you!

This law of sowing and reaping is one of God's
eternal principles. Weeds of worry, unclean thoughts,
fear and sin seem to spring up without being sown and
yet probably, without realising it, we have allowed
these seeds to be dropped into our minds. You might
see an advertisement on television for research into
some deadly disease. The announcer says: 'One out of
every ten people has this disease. *You may be that one.*
Help us fight . . .'
  This thought gets hold of you: 'I might be that one

who has that disease.' You start looking for symptoms and if you do not get rid of this thought, then it can take hold of you and can actually bring disease into your body. Doctors tell us that worry, anxiety, fear and depression lower our resistance to disease. Dr Taylor, of Columbia, South Carolina, said: 'I've never had a case of arthritis among black or white people, except among those who fear or are worried.'

In Job 3,25, we read: 'For the thing which I greatly feared is come upon me, and that which I was afraid of is come unto me.' Was this one of the reasons for Job's problems? Was Job full of worry and fear, dreading that the blessings he had received could not last? Did his fear draw negative results into his life? Did his worry and fear cause the hedge which God had placed around him to be broken down? These thoughts are worth considering.

Like an acorn dropping from an oak, taking root and growing into a new tree, so thoughts which are not done away with will drop from our mind into our hearts (our spirit) and take root. A worry-seed will bring forth a worry-tree with all of its deadly fruit, if we do not pluck it out.

Did you ever read the story: 'Little leopards become big leopards'? A native killed a mother leopard but took her cub home and kept it for a pet. The Chief of the village warned him that it would later become dangerous. All the people laughed, and said how sweet the little leopard was, it wouldn't kill a mouse! The man fed the leopard on porridge, so that it would not get a taste for meat and blood, and fondled it like a kitten.

The children played with the leopard as it got older and rode on its back; the Chief repeatedly warned them, but his words went unheeded. One day a small child fell in some thorn bushes and began to cry. The leopard ran up and began to lick the scratches on his legs and arms.

Suddenly, the fur on the leopard's back stood up; its eyes lost their soft look and became full of deadly hatred. A deep roar rose out of its throat and it bounded off towards the village. All the people fled, screaming in terror, and a well-shot arrow from the chief got rid of the leopard, but not before it had attacked and killed its former owner.

'*Little* leopards become *big* leopards.' *Little* worries become *big* worries. They must not be allowed to stay in our lives, or the day will come when they will overwhelm and destroy us. The longer we allow our worries to stay in our heart, the stronger their roots will become. Just like dandelion roots which go deep down in the soil searching for water and are so difficult to dig out, so our worries put deep roots down into our nature. These worry roots entwine in our thinking patterns, spawn fear-seeds in our heart and paralyse our faith and creativity.

Start planting a different kind of seed. Seeds of faith; seeds of God's promises; seeds of love and truth; seeds of trust; seeds of honesty and obedience; seeds of righteousness and cheerfulness. Let the powerful 'fertiliser' of the blood of Jesus cleanse and enrich the ground of your heart, that weeds and stubborn roots will find it impossible to stay there.

Watch over your new harvest with jealous care. Like the parable of the sower which Jesus told, there are enemies which will try to destroy the Word of God and this good harvest. The cares and pleasures of this world will try to choke the wheat with their thorns: the stones of bitterness and disappointment will keep the seed superficial and without depth of root, if not cleared from the ground; the birds of the air — Satan and his demon forces will try to attack and peck out the seed before it can even take root; the merciless sun of affliction and sorrow will dry the ground and scorch the tender shoots.

Remember, what you put into the strudel comes out

to be eaten; what you sow in the ground of your life will reproduce its kind. Check the seed you are sowing. If it has been good seed, watch over it with faith and patience, and 'in due season you will reap, if you faint not'.

If your seed has been bad, stop the harvest, annul it in the Name of Jesus. Begin to plant good, positive seed. Water it well with thanksgiving and the day will come when you and others will abundantly eat the good fruits you have brought forth.

15

The Power of the Name

Not only do we worry about the past and the situations we are in today, but we worry about the future — this great unknown monster which is lurking round the corner, drawing us nearer and nearer with every minute that passes.

Our younger generation is often known as the 'no-future' generation. Not only is the future 'unknown' but they are afraid there will be no future at all for them. Like generations in the past they have the normal worries of school exams, pimples on their faces, and the girls' torments that their faces and figures are not what they should be. But *our* young people are worried that there will be no jobs, that the politicians will blow us all up with atomic bombs, or that, even if the earth did remain, there would be no wildlife and vegetation because of pollution.

These are very real problems and if we did not know our Bibles which tell us something else, then we would have cause to worry.

In spring of 1987 we received a newsletter from a Dutch friend of ours. He travels often into Eastern Europe, preaching and helping the Christians there. He told the story of a Russian farmer who is in charge of a kolchose — a collective farm — not far from Tschernobyl. On this farm he has the care of 2,000 cows, 400 horses, and a large number of small livestock, and grows wheat, potatoes, strawberries and vegetables.

After the explosion of the nuclear power station *Nicolai was very worried. Many people were leaving the area, others lost their jobs and it was said that 20,000 pregnant women suffered miscarriages. Nicolai and his wife are both Christians (although Nicolai was more a 'secret' disciple than his wife) and he remembered a sermon about blessing people and things in the Name of Jesus. He determined to try this out.

Before he left to milk the 2,000 cows at 5 a.m. Nicolai blessed his pregnant wife and the whole house in the Name of Jesus. Then he blessed the cows, horses and livestock. He went over the farm and stretching his hands out over the crops, cried out: 'I bless you in the Name of Jesus!' This took him until noon. He even went down in the cellar and blessed all the eggs there, and blessed all the woodland around the farm.

Three days later some officials from the Ministry of Health came with their instruments to measure the level of radioactivity.

The farmer took them over the kolchose, to all the animals and lastly into his home, but there was not a trace of radioactivity. This was also the same at the farms where five other Christians had blessed their fields.

The official was dumbfounded and asked the sixty-four-thousand dollar question: 'How did you do it?' The farmer replied: 'My wife prays. It is her God that has done this!' Because the products were so good, the official bought meat, milk and eggs from the farmer, as they were the only ones in the district which were not contaminated.

Nicolai had carried out a spiritual experiment and found that blessing in the Name of Jesus can reverse radioactive contamination, one of the most dreaded evils of our modern-day world.

When the explosion occurred at Tschernobyl I was

*Name changed

98

in England, preaching. Helen and the children were at home in Germany and she told me what happened. High levels of radiation were reported all over Europe and especially in Scandinavia. People went into a panic and Tschernobyl was the talk of the day. Housewives bought up nearly all the tinned food in the shops and there was hardly any milk left because all the 'longlife milk' had been bought, too. The milk from the cows which had been grazing in the fields showed a high level of radiation, also the eggs from free-range chickens. People were scared to drink the water and were warned not to go out when it was raining because the radioactive dust was coming down from the clouds with the rain. Football and playing fields were measured and if the radiation was above a certain level, no games were allowed. Parents were advised not to let their children play in sandpits and many pregnant women were terrified lest their babies should be born deformed. Some even had abortions for this reason. Millions of lettuces and other fresh vegetables were declared unfit for sale, and people were afraid to eat their home-grown produce. Deer and other game had an especially high level of radiation for several months after the explosion.

However, during this time of panic there were Christians who committed their lives into the hands of their Heavenly Father; dug up the vegetables in their garden, prayed over them and ate them as usual.

The Bible tells us that in the last days mens' hearts will 'fail them for fear', and the scare from Tschernobyl gave us a foretaste of this. This was worry not only on a personal level but on a nation-wide, continent-wide and world-wide level.

Nicolai learnt the power in the Name of Jesus Christ and brought blessing and life to his household and area. I am reminded of a young man who also knew the power of 'the Name of the Lord' and brought deliverance to the whole of his nation.

This was David, the son of Jesse who, about 3,000 years ago, went to visit his brothers in the army. He found the king and all the soldiers trembling in terror at the Philistines' champion, the giant Goliath. Every day, for 40 days, Goliath shouted his challenge, but no one had the courage to go out and fight him.

David was a young lad about 17 years of age, and his blood boiled when he saw 'this uncircumcised Philistine who would dare to defy the armies of the living God'. He determined to fight Goliath and taking his shepherd's sling and five stones, went out to meet the giant. Goliath despised this young 'whippersnapper' and thought he was easy prey, but he had underestimated David.

The psychological slanging match continued with Goliath shouting he would give David's flesh to the birds and animals to eat, but David had a 'secret weapon' which Goliath knew nothing about, and he was not bothered.

'You come to me with a sword, and with a spear and with a shield: but I come to you in *the name of the Lord* of hosts, the God of the armies of Israel, whom you have defied. This day will the Lord deliver you into my hand; and I will smite you and take your head from you . . . And all this assembly shall know that the Lord saves not with sword and spear: for the battle is the Lord's and he will give you into our hands . . .' (1 Sam.17,45-47).

David ran to meet the giant, slung his stone and Goliath fell to the ground. Taking the giant's own sword he cut off his head, and the Philistines fled before the armies of Israel.

David might not have had a sword, but he knew the 'power of the name'. He did not know the name of *Jesus,* for Jesus did not come to earth until several hundred years later. Even then, the name Jesus in all its power and ability to set captives free did not come into force until Jesus died and rose again from the dead.

Because Jesus humbled himself in becoming a man and a servant, because he was obedient unto death, even the death of the cross, 'God has highly exalted him and given him a name which is above every name: that at the name of Jesus every knee should bow, of things in heaven, of things in the earth, and things under the earth (i.e. angels, men and demons); and that every tongue should confess that Jesus Christ is Lord to the glory of God the Father . . .' (Philippians 2,7-11).

The power in the name of the Lord was David's 'secret weapon' and this power was then bestowed upon the name of Jesus, so that every Christian might be able to use this weapon against the giants which would stand in their path.

Suppose David had given in to worry and fear, like King Saul and the Israelite army; he could have prayed like we do sometimes: 'O Lord, you see this great giant. He's huge and he's frightening the life out of us all. I don't know what we're going to do! And you know Lord, I've never fought a giant before. I'm not even a soldier or trained to fight. Why don't *you* go and fight him for us, Lord? That would be best . . .'

Did David pray like that? No! He went boldly forth and taking the Name won a mighty victory for the whole of the nation of Israel. If they had waited for God to fight Goliath, they would still be waiting. God expected them to do what they could, in his power, as he directed, and he would see to the rest.

Have *you* discovered the power in this name? Have you *personally* used it to pull down the strongholds of difficulties and problems Satan has raised up in your life? If not, begin to study how the apostles used the name of Jesus to bring deliverance and healing; find out what the name of Jesus can do for you. It is in this name *alone* that we can be saved (Acts 4,12), the name he obtained by conquest and through inheritance from his Father (Hebrews 1,4). Take this marvellous name and use it in faith *today!*

16

Take the 'Long Look'

I noticed the rose for the first time that morning. Of course, we must have passed it every day, going down the steps outside the Pension Chalet in Switzerland where Helen and I were spending our honeymoon. One thousand metres below, the blue waters of Lake Thun sparkled like glittering diamonds in the sun and the snow-capped Niesen mountain, a local tourist attraction, stood like a majestic pyramid in the background.

But that morning as I lay sunbathing on the grass and opened my eyes, the first thing I saw was the rose — a nest of dark red, delicate, velvet petals. It was not just its beauty that captivated me, but it was the fact that it seemed larger than the whole of the Thun Lake with its villages clustering on the shores; larger than the Niesen! But that was impossible, for the lake was miles long and the Niesen thousands of feet high. The rose was only about four inches in diameter. The difference was that I was so *near* to the rose. It filled my vision down on the grass, although in actual fact it was much smaller than the objects which were farther away.

I had passed that rose every day and it was swallowed up in the whole of the magnificent view, unnoticed. But it suddenly became important to me when I got down close to it. Not just that, it even seemed larger than everything else.

We may overlook certain things in life and they

don't trouble us too much, but if they suddenly become acute we are painfully aware of them. They stand out like a sore thumb and we worry and fret; nothing else matters except our problem. The problem may not be all that great, but our worrying magnifies it to such an extent that it fills our vision.

Something that concerns us or our family hits us far more than when the same thing happens to somebody else. An earthquake in Mexico or the famine in Ethiopia is not as awful to you as your aching tooth or the car keys you lost that morning. Although your tooth or car keys are not as devastating as the earthquake or famine, yet to you personally, they seem far worse.

We need to learn to see beyond our immediate problems or the thing that causes us to worry and be anxious, for that will help us to get things in proportion and gain the right perspective.

Seen in the light of the end result our greatest worries, which look larger than life, take on other proportions and pale into insignificance. Instead of giving way to panic and sleepless nights, we realise that this problem will not always be there. We are passing *through* and life moves on. The car keys will be found or you can have new ones made. Your aching tooth can be treated, and painful though the procedure may be, it will soon be over.

This principle is also true in things which face us that are far worse than lost car keys or aching teeth. There is the doctor's verdict that there is little hope; a teenage son or daughter breaking your heart by their rebellion; a pile of bills which you have no way of paying. In each situation, we must look beyond the immediate problem to God's intervention, his help and his plans for us.

When Jesus was facing the excruciating agony of death by crucifixion, he looked beyond the experience to the joy and triumph of his resurrection. Death and the cross lasted just a few hours but their results will last for eternity.

'He, for the joy (of obtaining the prize) that was set before Him, endured the cross, despising and ignoring the shame, and is now seated at the right hand of the throne of God,' (Hebrews 12,2. Amplified Bible).

Moses, who had been brought up as an Egyptian prince, turned his back on this life of luxury and chose to become a nomad in the desert as God's chosen leader for the Israelite slaves. We can see the reason for his choice in Hebrews 11,26 and 27:

'He considered the contempt and abuse and shame (borne for) the Christ, the Messiah (who was to come), to be greater wealth than all the treasures of Egypt, for he looked *forward and away* to the reward (recompense). Motivated by faith he left Egypt behind him, being unawed and undismayed by the wrath of the king; for he never flinched but held staunchly to his purpose and endured steadfastly as one who gazed on Him who is invisible,' (Amplified Bible).

Moses took 'the long look'. He looked beyond the pleasures of Egypt and the difficulties with the Children of Israel, realising that the reward of obeying God was far greater than anything he would encounter in this life.

Yet when we are in times of great difficulty or sorrow, no one can say it is easy to get things in perspective and to 'look away and beyond'. These occasions come to us all, to a lesser or greater degree, and the temptation to worry, fear or panic is enormous.

There is a verse in Isaiah 43,2 that I have found very comforting: 'When you pass through the waters, I will be with you: and through the rivers, they shall not overflow you; when you walk through the fire, you will not be burned; neither shall the flame kindle upon you (set you alight)'.

God is saying here 'when', not 'if'. In other words, he shows us that life brings testings and difficult hours as well as sunshine. 'When' you go through these situations, know that I am with you, he is reminding us.

Your problems may be so overwhelming that you feel like a man who is standing in water and feels it rising, rising higher, and he is powerless to do anything to stop it. Any moment now, and the waters will close over his head and he'll be swept away. But God says: It will not be like that with you — 'the waters will *not* overflow you', and even though you feel as if you are in a furnace of sorrow and affliction, although you may feel their heat, the flames will *not* be able to burn and destroy you.

Another comforting thought in this verse is that we are going *'through'*. It is a temporary situation. It will not last a lifetime. Your time of trial may be a few weeks or even months and years, yet the time will come when you will have reached the other side. God is telling us here to remember to 'take the *long look*; take courage, behind those clouds my sun is shining; I am working although you may not see the result yet; let's cross this river *together*; let's walk *through* the fire *together*. You are going to make it. Don't give in to worry and fear, but put your hand in mine and trust me.'

This makes me think of Job, the main character in the oldest book in the Bible, of the same name. Job was the richest man in the land and a very upright and God-fearing man, but one day calamity after calamity began to strike him. Job did not know that in the spiritual, unseen world the stage was being set for one of the greatest dramas of all time. It all started with Satan being jealous of the worship Job gave to God, and God's favour upon this man. Satan declared that if God removed all the things in Job's life which he held dear, Job would curse God and turn from him.

This had been Satan's problem from the beginning. Pride and jealousy made him try to *outdo* God, but we know how this former angel was thrust out of Heaven.

Then in Job's case, Satan thought he *knew* more than God, but he is not omniscient, all-knowing. God still reigns supreme. At the cross, Satan thought he had *outwitted* God by nailing his son there, but that was the Father's purpose from the beginning of time! After the millenium Satan in his final deadly battle will try to 'out-fight' God, and he won't win there either!

But of course Job did not know all this for he came upon the stage in the second act, and had not heard the conversation between God and Satan. Being a well-known man, he is now in the public gaze more than ever. It is the talk of the town how Job has lost his children, his livestock and now his health. Only his wife remains, but she adds the last straw to break the camel's back by telling Job to 'curse God and die'.

It seemed that the devil was pulling all the strings with Job dangling like a helpless puppet. But in fact, God was still backstage, writing the script to turn things around for Job. God believed in Job, just as he believes in you! God had faith in Job and had not forsaken him. An onlooker would have said: 'Job, you're finished,' but God said: 'Come on Job, let's go *through* this thing together. Look *beyond* it.'

When we look at the world, it surely seems in a mess, but Satan's lease (which was given to him by Adam and Eve's sin) is nearly running out, and God is going to wind up the affairs of this world in *his* way. He is getting ready to write Earth's final chapters, and is taking 'the long look'.

Bible scholars believe that what is described in the book of Job, took place in about one or two years. God turned the captivity of Job, and gave him twice as many riches as before and ten more children. His daughters were the most beautiful girls around and, together with their brothers, Job gave them an inheritance. Then to cap it all, Job lived another 140 years in the best of health, and saw his grandchildren come into the world.

Your life may seem very tangled, like the back of a carpet or piece of embroidery. The threads go cross-cross, the colours are dull and lifeless, there is no system or reason; but remember, it's not finished yet. Start to 'take the long look'; start to see with God's eyes. He knows what he is doing. One day you will be able to see the pattern on the right side. It will be beautiful, meaningful, a delight to him, and you will be able to see that your Father knew what he was doing.

What I don't understand I'll just leave in his hand
He'll show me the way I should go.
I'll not worry and fret and just try to forget
About the things I should know.
One day I shall see that he led me aright
So I'll trust where I can't always trace.
Then upon my path will continually shine
The light from his wonderful face!

Helen

17

People under Pressure

Two of our modern-day evils are *loneliness* and *pressure*. High-rise blocks of flats appear to many people as little cages or boxes where humans are shut in, and the bare, grey concrete of much modern 'architecture' leaves us feeling cold, stripped and threatened, as if the passage walls will close in upon us.

It is possible for us to be in a crowd of people and yet to feel as if we are on a desert island, marooned and shut off from the rest of the world; nobody understands how we feel or has time to try to make contact with us. Loneliness can come from physical withdrawal or because the rest of the world is 'under pressure' and they don't seem concerned.

People hurry by and have no time to notice; our world runs on schedules, appointments, dinner on the table when the family gets home, and deadlines which must be met.

Necessary as all these things are, we can become like Martha if we are not careful. She wanted to make a scrumptious meal for Jesus and all the guests, but became worked up and lost her inward peace. Jesus commended Mary because she took time to sit and hear his words.

How easy it is to be so caught up in the pressures in life that we neglect to take time with Jesus, or time for others. Often we go heedlessly along not realising that the people around us, even someone very close — our husband or wife — may need us to take time to listen to their problems.

The Bible tells us to 'bear one another's burdens and so fulfil the law of Christ'. Our understanding of each other must deepen; our sensitivity to others' needs must become finer and we must learn to communicate more freely. What is a problem to you may seem ridiculous to me; what is perplexing me at this moment may never have entered your mind. We are all so individual that it is sometimes good to put ourself in the other person's position, and see things from his point of view. When worries weight us down and we cannot share them with anyone, it seems as if a great loneliness is trying to engulf us.

Take the Christian businessman, trying to live as he believes God would have him to, while his colleagues laugh at his integrity, truth and clean living. Inflation, taxes, competition, falling sales, heart trouble through stress, younger men trying to take his place, Japanese products flooding the market, and countless other problems seek to overwhelm him.

Then there is the overworked mother coping with a stream of runny noses, dirty nappies and too many toddlers under her feet, and the fear that she is pregnant again. Her husband is about to lose his job, he's too often on the bottle and she is sure he has a girl-friend — she saw lipstick on his handkerchief and a blonde hair on his jacket lapel. When she looks at the women on television, beautifully groomed and with a figure like the goddess Diana, she is just about ready to give up.

Then there is the fear of getting old, of being helpless with arthritis or some other disease, of being unwanted and becoming a querulous, pain-ridden O.A.P., of being unwanted by relatives, perhaps widowed, just waiting to die, living in the memories of the past, because the present holds so little joy.

Then there is the pressure of chronic illness or of having a sick or handicapped child; the struggle to live a normal life; the fear of treatment and doctors and what decision to make. The bitterness and frustration of 'why did it have to happen to us'.

There is the young wife who has lost her baby and cannot have any more. Years of childless marriage stretch out before her and she yearns to cradle a child in her arms, longs for family life and feels a 'second-class' woman in comparison to the mums in the park, proudly pushing prams. How can so many have abortions?

There are the politicians, faced with problems of such magnitude as never before. The minister with problems in his church. There's no one he can turn to — he is supposed to be the man with the answers! He is not supposed to have any personal needs. His children should be models of perfection and nobody knows his wife feels she is pulled a thousand ways, trying to live up to everybody's expectations.

People all around us are worried and under pressure, and Helen and I have had many such crises. Just now while we are writing this book, for example.

In just a few days I shall be leaving for an itinerary in England, Scotland and Ireland. Helen wanted to compile a book of her poems which we suddenly realised should come out before I leave. I started to type them out for the printer when our electric typewriter started to play up. Sometimes I had to press the same letter six times before it would type!

If we had had a computer to centralise the poems and titles, Bible-texts, etc., it would have been an enormous help, but we had to do it the old-fashioned way: counting letters, spaces, and measuring to get the poems in the right place on the page. We finished at 2 a.m., two days after it should have gone to the printer.

While doing this poetry typing (62 pages) I have been helping to organise the 'Euro-Vision '88' conference. This has involved many messages by telefax, telephone conversations to England, USA, Sweden and throughout Germany, with delays and difficulties of many kinds. Time is running out.

The conference is to be at the beginning of August and it is now already the third week in April. People under pressure!

Both Helen and I have been speaking at separate meetings in the last three weeks, and I've been making final arrangements for my itinerary in the United Kingdom, and there were some changes that had to be made concerning my boat ticket to Ireland. As usual, one detail ties in with another, and until you receive the information about A, B and C, you cannot decide on what to do concerning G. Sometimes E and F will sort themselves out, but until A, B, C and D are certain, you cannot work out your final result of A, B, C, D, E, F and G.

It is in these times of pressure that we are tempted to panic, but if we take time to listen for the inward witness of God's Spirit, he will guide us in practical details in a miraculous way. Often we must 'stand still' and then we shall 'see the salvation of the Lord'.

This book is almost finished (Helen has four more chapters to write) and we had hoped to give a publisher the whole manuscript at the end of April. There's only one problem: it's written by hand and I still have to type out about 21 chapters, and do a hundred other things before leaving on the 28 April for England. It's 'people under pressure'.

Then there was the time when we had just moved from Frankfurt to south Germany and I was doing two radio broadcasts every week, taping them in a studio nearby. The broadcasts had to be sent several weeks in advance to the radio station and due to various circumstances we were 'under pressure' and late again.

Just then we received the news that Helen's father was very ill; could we come? We rushed to pack and made last-minute arrangements, and arrived two days later. For the next three weeks we visited Helen's father in the hospital every day and tried to work on these radio broadcasts. I wrote them in German for the German broadcasts and Helen translated them for the English programmes. Each sermon had to be clearly typed out so that they could be easily read.

One night the house next door caught fire. We all tumbled out of bed shivering, packed Helen's mother and the children into the car and drove up the road away from the row of houses as there was danger of a gas explosion. Kind neighbours invited us in and put on tea and biscuits for us at 3 a.m. with true English comradeship, and the firemen managed to get the fire under control fairly quickly. But . . . it was just a bit more pressure.

Helen's father was declining rapidly and it was a grief to see him so ill, but life had to go on. We struggled with the radio messages — 18 in all, each three foolscap pages long — and then I had to race to a studio in Eastbourne to make the actual broadcasts, and get the tapes sent off to Portugal to the radio station.

Just about the time when we had originally planned to come to England, Helen's father died. His last words to Helen and me on the previous evening had been 'Jesus is wonderful'. That same morning our son Paul, who was then seven years old, gave his life to Jesus. He had been listening to some of my radio broadcasts on cassettes. These messages and knowing that 'Grandad was soon going to be with Jesus', along with a picture of 'The Rapture' with people rising to meet the Lord in the air made a great impression on him, and he wanted to be saved, too. One life was snuffed out but another one was lit on that day, and God gave us joy in the midst of pressures and grief.

Some people work well under pressure and accomplish more than if everything was jogging along at a steady pace. It is astonishing what we can do when we have to. Nevertheless, our bodies and minds were not made to *live* under stress and pressure. We can manage for a while but then we begin to have problems.

Helen and I have worked for various Christian organisations and often there were no regular working hours. There were certain things that had to be done and if it took four hours or 14 hours it made no difference.

In one mission where we worked, an annoying thing was that a certain plan would be decided upon, arrangements would be made with different countries, printers, financing and a dozen other details, then suddenly the plan would be changed. All our former work was scrapped. Hours or weeks of work were wasted and we would have to nearly kill ourselves to meet the deadline date.

For instance, it was decided that a large printing job should be done in Hong Kong because it was much cheaper than Europe. However, several details were overlooked and the whole project was not planned carefully enough. Because of the great distance geographically, communication was difficult, and the printers there did not understand the instructions or the language of the material which was to be printed. When the proofs were sent to us to be corrected the whole thing was in such a mess, we had to cancel the order. Much time, money and effort had been wasted, and the books were then printed in Germany, after all.

One weekend, all the European workers and their families of this particular mission were invited to a retreat in Austria. It was a time of teaching, sharing and relaxation. We also had some group discussions and one of the allocated questions was: 'Should we as Christians only work set hours, or should we be prepared to work until the job is done?'

We all realised that this had been brought up because of the many occasions (or constant policy of this mission!) to run things under 'M.B.C.' — 'Management By Crisis', thereby placing great strains on the personnel and their families.

Our group discussed the pros and cons of this policy and one young woman said: 'Jesus often didn't have time to eat or sleep, and didn't have any home life. So it shouldn't matter what hours we keep when we're working for the Lord.' To which Helen replied:

'How many years did Jesus minister? About three! We have a whole lifetime in front of us and if we want to give our best, we dare not be burned out before we are 30. And Jesus did not have any family. He worked at the carpenter's bench until he was 30 and then packed everything concentratedly into these three years. Then it was over. Each of us must often be prepared to "go the second mile" as we have proved we are willing to do, but we need to get some other priorities straight.'

The highest priority we need to set is our communion and time with our Lord. We must 'abide' in him and his words 'abide' in us. This means setting everything aside and being determined to follow as Jesus shows you; to do things in the order that he leads; to learn to say 'No' when people would push and insist you do certain things, when you know that God is leading you another way.

It is difficult to do this, and we are not always successful. We often get caught up in a whirl of activity and little time. I find this especially when I am on an itinerary. There are long distances to be covered by car, and road works and traffic jams threaten to make you late for your meeting or appointment. You preach and pray for people afterwards, sell books and cassettes, talk with the pastor, and then, at the house where you stay the night, people sometimes want to talk for several hours.

Once I went to stay with two elderly spinsters. I was tired after a long journey and the meeting, and longed for some peace and quiet. Suddenly the ladies' dog rushed in like a tornado, raced round and round the settee where I was sitting, taking a nip at my ankles as he passed. When I tried to ward him off, the ladies roared with laughter and protested that he was only being playful! Such a darling! . . .

Then next day, off we go again to another place. It is wonderful to be able to pray in the car and fellowship with the Lord, and long journeys are marvellous for this, but we need to guard our times of quiet and prayer. Our work and activities for Jesus mean nothing if they do not spring from our *inner* life and love for Jesus. In the Bible college I attended a little plaque hanging over the doorway, read:

'Help me to love Thee more than Thy service'. What we do in service for God is important; but what we *are* is more important.

When worries and pressures would drag us down, we need to keep an ear open to God more than ever before. It is then we need God's wisdom to know what to do. 'My thoughts are higher than your thoughts; my ways are higher than your ways' he tells us in Isaiah 55, 8 and 9. We should seek God's wisdom even as we would seek for precious silver or gold. He has promised to give it to us.

Do not be bullied by pressure. Take a few minutes off; do something entirely different from the job in hand. Go for a walk; arrange flowers; listen to some good music; read something inspiring, comforting or humorous; make love; paint a picture; play or sing; watch the sunset; weed a flower bed; pray and worship; bake a cake. You will be refreshed and able to go on better afterwards.

If possible, take one thing at a time. If this is not possible and you must tackle several jobs together, try to keep your inner peace; work like Martha if you must, but cultivate Mary's attitude and spirit, and you'll *hold* up, not *fold* up under pressure.

18

How to Defeat Discouragement

Some of the greatest men of God in the Bible prayed to die. It is a real comfort to know that when we are facing such times, we are not alone. Most of us have at some-time or another walked in the wilderness of discouragement. But very few have tasted the dregs of discouragement, where praying to die seemed the only way out.

Elijah was one of these few men. He had soared to the greatest height of his career as the whole nation of Israel saw God confirming his prayer on Mount Car-mel. The fire fell and consumed not only the sacrifice but the stones as well. It was no doubt an outstanding victory. The people shouted: 'The Lord he is the God, the Lord he is the God'. Running before Ahab's horses as the hand of the Lord came upon him, a distance of nearly 20 miles, was another triumph.

Suddenly the victory of Carmel is overshadowed by a message from Queen Jezebel, who threatens to take his life. Previously Elijah dared to stand up to the king but now fear, fatigue, nervous tension and discourage-ment forced him to make a panic decision. At the beginning of his ministry every step he took was directed by the Lord; he obeyed in going to the brook, and the widow's home, but in this case he had no time to ask for further guidance. Driven by fear, he ran a distance of over 80 miles to Beersheba. Not content with this, he left his servant there and went a day's journey into the wilderness, and sat down under a

117

juniper tree.

Away from the glare of publicity, he had time to think. '. . . It is enough; now, O Lord, take away my life.' But if he had really wanted to die, Queen Jezebel would have obliged. Elijah had reached the lowest ebb of his life, he had exchanged Carmel's victory for the despair of the wilderness; self-pity and discouragement had taken over.

Here he sits dejected, discouraged, frustrated and lonely. His prayer is not that of a man of God but of one who is under the hypnotic drug of discouragement.

Elijah had a 'pity party' all by himself. Normally we like to have people around us so that they can pity us — 'Oh, you poor thing . . .' It makes us feel so good.

Exhausted, Elijah fell asleep. Maybe he wished that he would die in his sleep — this would have been the easiest way out. But he was shocked by an angel bringing his breakfast, and later, another meal, on the strength of which he went 40 days and nights without food.

Elijah's prayer to die was not answered. Why? Because God knows the real motive behind this kind of praying!

I heard Lance Lambert mention the following point about Elijah. 'Just because an angel fries your breakfast for you does not mean you are going in the right direction!' The further Elijah went — even to Horeb — the greater the distance he had to cover coming back.

A journey set in motion by discouragement will never fulfil God's perfect plan. God's question to Elijah at Horeb: 'What are you doing here, Elijah?' shows us that he should never have been there at all. God's reply to him was: 'Go, return . . .'

There are many things in our lives that would try to discourage us. Discouragement comes for various reasons. What are *you* discouraged about today? Have you children hooked on drugs or problems in your marriage? Has your wife an incurable disease? Have you financial worries or cannot find a job? Are you disappointed with your church? Are you lonely and have no one to turn to? Perhaps God has not answered your prayer or you feel life is passing you by. The list is endless. You can insert your own type of discouragement. So, how can we defeat discouragement?

King David fought and won many battles. However, one of his greatest battles was not with giants but with discouragement. 1 Sam.30 gives us insight into this situation. The Amalekites had invaded Ziklag, burned the city, and taken David's wives and children captive. His own men were getting ready to stone him, and David had no one to turn to or to encourage him. He could have become bitter and blamed God for this situation. How often we blame God for things he has never done. God gets blamed for the things that the devil does. Sometimes we blame God for the foolish things we do.

The 'feeling' area of our life is so fickle. It changes quicker than the weather. This is the hardest area in which to get the victory. How did David feel in this predicament? The pressure was on. What should he do? His men's impatience was increasing by the minute. His pulse raced against time. David and his people had wept for so long that they had no more power to weep and he was in great distress.

In the midst of this dramatic setting we read the following words, '. . . but *David encouraged himself in the Lord his God*' (1 Samuel 30 v 6).

Little did David know during that time that these words would encourage millions throughout the centuries facing similar situations. His greatest battle was with *himself!*

Many things had to be overcome before David could begin to encourage himself in the Lord. He also could have prayed to die. Again this would have been the easiest way out. He could have run off and left the problem behind, or have allowed self-pity to take over, and discouragement would have been glad to help him.

David could have tried many things but instead he did something that in the natural seemed foolish, yet it was the solution for his problem. It is good to receive encouragement from others, in meetings through the preached Word of God. It is quite easy to give encouragement to others, but the hardest is to encourage *yourself*. Have you tried it?

How did David encourage himself? I am sure that he began to think back to the times when God had helped him; the lion, bear and the battle with Goliath. As he meditated on these things faith began to rise up within him. Yes, God will help me again. I can have victory in this situation! That's why discouragement is such a great enemy to our faith. It stops us expecting God to act. Through discouragement we *defeat ourselves!* Encouraging himself in the Lord gave David clarity to act. He asked the Lord for guidance and the battle was won (1 Samuel 30).

The whole situation was changed because David encouraged himself in the Lord. Discouragement is not the answer. It will rob us of the victories that God has planned for us. Arise from your discouragement and self-pity and encourage yourself in Jesus. Life will be worth living again. Jesus is waiting to help you take your first step out of discouragement. It is a matter of your will!

We have the choice — to allow discouragement or encouragement to dominate us. When discouraged we cannot smile and have a long face, but when Jesus has helped us to overcome discouragement, everything changes and we can say with the Psalmist: 'He will make me smile again' (Psalm 43 v 5 Living Bible).

We must be very careful how we act when we are in the grip of discouragement. This is not the time to make important decisions, life-changing plans. Discouragement causes us to see everything black and distorted. We cannot see or think clearly at such times.

We have heard of people being so discouraged that they have rushed off and divorced their husband or wife, and regretted it for the rest of their life. Others give up their job, women have abortions, the desperate are driven to suicide when prolonged discouragement leads to depression and despair.

Remember you are not the only one who has ever been discouraged. Circumstances come to us almost every day which give us the opportunity to be discouraged. Every human being has had the chance to be depressed, and some of the world's greatest men and women have had to fight this giant.

Discouragement is another weapon from the devil's arsenal which he loves to use against God's children. Not only do we ourselves become discouraged but it seems that in every church there is somebody who has this special 'ministry of discouragement' which they use against others. I have seen these people in Europe and the UK, some in America and over in India. Whenever a new project is being discussed, these people are sure it will never work. The pastor encourages the new converts, but as soon as his back is turned the discouragers start to pour their doubts and discouraging words into the converts' ears. We should seek to *encourage* and build up each other, not pull down and ridicule everything that is being accomplished for God.

When I was in the Bible college, one eager young student prayed: 'O Lord, water the heavenly spark'.

I wondered if the Lord was amused at this mix-up of metaphors, but it reminded me of those discouragers who are always ready with the water hose, pouring cold water on every spark of activity and blessing in the church. Anybody can criticise. Criticism is cheap. It is far easier to sit as a spectator and make fun of those who are running a marathon, than to get out there on the track and sweat it out.

When David went to kill Goliath, his brothers ridiculed him; the king told him he couldn't do it, and Goliath scorned him. But David was not impressed; he closed his ears to their criticism and won the day.

We often see pictures of Peter sinking in the water, but how often does an artist portray him walking on the water, which is what he actually did. What were the disciples thinking when he stepped out of the boat? — 'The fellow's crazy. Typical of Peter! I knew he would take it too far.' Human nature tends to play good things down, to be negative and pessimistic, to discourage rather than encourage.

Therefore, discouragement comes at us from two fronts; the inward discouragement which comes from what we see and feel or through a definite attack from Satan, and the outward discouragement which other people bring against us with their discouraging words.

God wants to bring us over to the side of the encourager and the encouraged — one who encourages others and one who, himself, is *encouraged*. Like David, if you have no one to encourage you, you can encourage yourself in the Lord and then in turn, look around for someone else to encourage. The way out of your need is not through the door of despair and doubt, but through the door of encouragement. And if you have been one of those with the 'ministry of discouragement', then bury this talent as soon as you can.

Just as a little thing can suddenly thrust an arrow of discouragement through a chink in your armour, so also can a little simple act of kindness encourage someone in need. Maybe just a smile when you pass the frail old lady in the supermarket, or a helping hand to the young mum with a brood of toddlers.

A grip of the hand and real warmth in your voice can make someone feel that they really have worth. Write a letter to a lonely missionary, make that telephone call you've been meaning to for so long. Tell the young man grappling with discouragement and depression he is going to make it, that he's not finished. Be an *Encourager* and see the encouragement *you* need flow back to you!

It may not be easy at first. The hardest part is always the start. When a train starts the wheels of the engine begin to move very slowly then gain in momentum and a new journey has begun.

The huge Boeing first taxis slowly across the tarmac at the airport terminal until it finds space to make its rush down the runway and shoot up into the sky. When I drive my car I cannot start in fourth gear; I must put the lever in position of first gear and only as I gather speed can the fourth be reached.

But without this *first* turning of the wheel, without this initial setting in motion, the journey of thousands of miles would not be possible. At first, when the wheels are moving very slowly, only a short distance is covered. But the faster the wheels go, the greater the output of the engine and the greater the distance that will be covered.

On your journey out of discouragement and worry, your progress may be slow at first. But keep at it. You are gaining speed. You are learning. Soon the dismal landscape of discouragement will be left behind, and you will be speeding through the meadows of trust, along the highway of faith and soaring up into the heavens of answered prayer!

Another great secret which helped David was the truth about 'praise'. Scores of the psalms encourage and *command* us to praise God; David's heart and harp were tuned in to the heavenly wavelength. He rejoiced in his God and was determined that all people should do the same.

When he brought up the ark of God there was great rejoicing, singing and playing of instruments, and David himself danced 'with all his might' in praise to

God. Not only on *this day* was God to be praised, but David ordered certain of the Levites to praise *'continually'* (24 hours a day) before the ark. They were to sing and play their instruments, and he chose men who were skilful, who would bring a beautiful praise-offering to God.

Praise was not solely for David; it is for us, too. One of the best ways to break worry and discouragement is to learn to praise God. Praising does not mean that I might be feeling in a good mood and so I start to sing choruses and hymns. Praising is not something I do because I *feel* good and everything is just fine. Praising is a matter of my *will*. I make the *decision* to praise God, or I make the decision *not* to praise him. David often said: 'I *will* praise the Lord . . .' He had made a *decision* to do it, in spite of his circumstances.

Praise delights God's heart and he is *worthy* to be praised. We should praise him for what he has done, but most of all for what he *is!* When our heart and thoughts are concentrating on praising him, this activity brings us out of the passive state of worry and discouragement. Circumstances will change; answers to prayer will suddenly arrive; doors which have remained stubbornly closed will fly open as God's army goes into action, winning victories on our behalf. Praise is a weapon in God's armoury which will often bring results where *prayer* has failed.

Paul and Silas praised at midnight, their feet in the stocks, their backs bleeding. Imprisoned for preaching the Gospel. All the prisoners could hear these crazy preachers singing, but God sent an earthquake; the prison walls crumbled and everybody's chains dropped off.

King Jehoshaphat wanted to do something to please God, so he sent a praising choir *in front of the army* as they went out to face the enemy, and God sent ambushments against their enemies for them. God had spoken to him earlier and said:

'Be not afraid nor dismayed by reason of this great multitude; for the battle is not yours, but God's . . . You shall not need to fight in this battle: set yourselves, stand still and see the salvation of the Lord with you . . . fear not, nor be dismayed . . .' (2 Chronicles 20, 15 to 17).

Jehoshaphat had believed this word from the Lord, and sent the praisers out, and the next thing they knew was that the enemy lay *dead* on the field.

We, too, must realise that the battle is the Lord's, and he wants to fight for us. But we must fulfil the conditions: *'Set yourselves, stand still . . .'* and that is the most difficult thing to do. Fear, dismay, worry and discouragement drive us to panic and to try desperately to find a way out of our situation. But Jehoshaphat obeyed, believed and magnified his God, and God fought the battle for him.

Praising is not something we should do occasionally, it should become a life-style for every Christian. We should make the decision to defeat discouragement and worry with praise.

We heard the true story of a lady missionary who was dying with smallpox. Out on a lonely mission post, without medical aid, death was inevitable. She had prayed and wept, but no answer came; she only grew worse. One day, as she lay praying, God gave her a vision. She saw a pair of scales with one side weighed down lower than the other. God showed her that on this heavy side of the scales was her grumbling, complaining and smallpox. On the lighter side was her 'praising'. She immediately realised what she had to do. She began to praise and thank God as never before, disregarding all physical symptoms and discomfort. The people who were looking after her, heard her praising God hour after hour, and thought the illness had affected her mind.

But the more she praised, the heavier the 'praise-side' of the scales became, and the lighter the 'grumbling side'. Soon she was out of her bed healed! She concentrated on the greatness of her God and on magnifying him, not on her need, and he intervened on her behalf.

It is easy to praise *after* we see the answer — anyone can do that. The real test is to do it *before* we see the victory, the solution to our problem. When we are in the dungeon of discouragement, loaded down with chains of problems, our feet in the stocks of human limitation — that is the time to praise and encourage ourselves in the Lord. The devil hates praisers of God; he would like us to praise what he has been doing, to look at the chaos he has wrought in our lives. But for those of us who are learning how to 'win over worry', we need to do as David did. When I was in the Bible college one of the lecturers put it this way: 'David took his soul out, looked down at it in his hand and began to speak to it:

"Why are you cast down, O my soul, my inner self? And why are you disquieted, so disturbed within me? *Hope in God* and wait expectantly for him; *for I shall yet praise him* who is the help of my countenance, and my God".' (Psalm 42,11, Amplified Bible)

Let us do the same!

19

Words can Make or Break You

Have you ever imagined what our world would be like without words?

For a start, there would not be any world here, for God spoke the earth and all of nature into being. He continued to use words by speaking to Adam and Eve, and they in turn taught this language to their children. Words were a means of communication between God and people and each other, to convey feelings and ideas.

Then there came the *written word,* where people began to make drawings or signs to communicate. This might have been on the wall of a cave, or scratched in a soft piece of clay or on Egyptian papyrus. These signs later became the various alphabets which are used today in different parts of the world, and give us our writing system.

God attaches the utmost importance to communication and words. He inspired men to write the Bible which brings to us the message of eternal life. He has written our names in the Book of Life and engraved them on the palms of his hands. The Ten Commandments were written by his finger on tablets of stone. Many prophets were told not only to tell the message God gave them, but to *write* it in a book.

Whereas animals and other creatures are able, in a very basic and instinctive way, to communicate, only to human beings — those made in the image of God — is given this power and ability to communicate with words and express ideas and feelings.

What would life be without these words? There would be total lack of understanding between people if they could not speak. There would never be a song written or heard, never a book, newspaper or love letter read. No radio or television; no church service could be held without words, etc.; no schools to train our children.

Very little would be invented or studied. Even practical objects, everyday things would be very limited as nobody would know how to make them or where to obtain the materials.

We are told that the average person speaks 30,000 words a day; these words would make a paperback if printed and within a few years we would have our own library.

The question is, what are we saying every day? Would you like the words which you spoke today to be front-page headlines on your local newspaper? 'Mrs Jones said . . . to her husband,' 'Mr Meredith criticises his pastor . . .' How embarrassing if this were to happen!

I read of a man who was always critising others. One day he visited some friends and they secretly turned on the cassette-player and recorded all he said. After about an hour, they told him they had a special tape, which would interest him. The tape was switched on and to the man's great chagrin, his own voice — harsh and critical — sounded through the room. All the latest church gossip and questionable titbits, the pastor and his failings were well and truly aired, and the man's face grew redder and redder. After a while he could stand it no longer and ran out of the house.

The article did not say whether this man learnt his lesson but let's hope he did. All of us need to watch our vocabulary and it always seems easier to speak out negative rather than positive things. A small spark can ignite a fire. This fire can be used for warmth, to cook sausages over, and to guard against wild animals. But the same fire in the wrong place, can bring destruction and death. The words we speak can also ignite fires, bringing warmth and comfort, or disappointment and death.

There are numerous Bible verses which show the importance of what we say. When we speak, we are not just allowing sounds to come out of our mouth; our words are an expression of what we believe, think or feel. They are containers with meaningful contents.

Every word I read or speak conjures up a picture in my mind. If I say: 'The chestnut tree needs chopping down. The branches are far too thick and it is shutting out the light from the house.' My mind continues to the next picture and I see the men coming to take down the tree, and later, the empty space.

That is a very simple illustration, but what if I spoke out words like: 'I'm sure to be one of those made redundant. I've seen it coming all along. We won't be able to pay our bills and there's no way we can get by.'

As you speak this, your mind sees the boss telling you you've lost your job; sees you walking into the house, depressed and worried, you telling your wife and she begins to cry. You see yourself at the employment agency; the lady shakes her head; no vacancies.

You pick up your dole money and it's so hard to get by. You are thinking of selling the house and feel worthless, helpless and angry because of your situation. Even as these thoughts are coming, you begin to feel the emotion brought on by these imagined pictures of depression, fear, anger and frustration.

But the situation has not even arisen! It may *never* arise, yet you are already imagining it, speaking it out and almost acting as if it had indeed already come!

When the Children of Israel heard the twelve spies give their report, their minds immediately visualised the giants, the huge, walled cities and they said: 'We can't go and take the land.' They were already tremb-

129

ling although the giants were miles away. Words produce an atmosphere, and the atmosphere of fear and defeat settled upon the Israelite camp.

Several years ago we stayed in the home of an ex-boxer, who is now a preacher. Our two boys, Paul and David, were asking him some questions about his years in the ring, and he made an interesting remark: 'One of the best ways to beat your opponent is to beat him psychologically first.'

This is what Goliath tried as he told David he would give his flesh to the birds and beasts of the field. Mohammed Ali was building up his image and using psychological pressure when he used to say: 'I'm the greatest!'

But there are some deeper truths here than just a psychological battle, powerful though it may sometimes be. The Bible talks of death and life being in the power of the tongue (Prov.18,21), and that the tongue acts to the body as a rudder to a ship (James 3, 4 and 5). James is saying here that a man who has learnt to control his tongue, to speak wisely and discreetly, will also be able to control his actions and desires.

At first sight this may seem unlikely, yet James, through the inspiration of the Holy Spirit, was writing a truth 2,000 years ago, which has been verified by medical science in our 20th century. Neurosurgeons tell us it has been discovered that the speech centre in the brain has total control over all the other nerves. They have found that the way we speak affects the rest of our body, and how the nerves react.

Have you ever seen a man coming up to retirement age? He is listless, has no energy or drive, and dreads the thought of not going to work any longer. He feels worthless, for the only contribution he has made to his world will soon be cut off. Life becomes meaningless. This happens to many men. They begin to speak out these feelings:

'I am retired now. I'm not worth anything. The days

are just dragging by. I feel weak and old. There is nothing worth looking forward to.' He withdraws into a cocoon of self-pity and resignation; his nerves begin to signal negative responses to his body. His mental and physical health begins to decline. He is less active and can eventually die sooner than necessary.

Instead of regarding retirement as an opportunity to open a new chapter in his life, a chance to do some of those things for which there was no time before, he is already counting himself out of the race and giving up.

How amazing that God has made our bodies like this! What a grave responsibility we have when we realise this; what marvellous opportunities when we see the potential here! What are you saying each day? Are you constantly speaking out worry-words, fear-words? If so, your speech nerve centre is then translating those negative responses throughout your body, and in time you will act accordingly.

Or are you speaking out words of faith, of confidence in your Heavenly Father, bringing harmony, health and well-being in your spirit, soul and body?

Christian Science teaches that all disharmony, sickness and sin is merely a state of mind. It teaches that if you *think* you are sick, then you *are* sick, but if you think you are *not* sick, then you are well. They deny the existence of sin and sickness, like the proverbial ostrich which puts its head in the sand. This is often referred to as 'mind over matter'.

How foolish and destructive this teaching is! If a person denies he is a sinner then he will think he has no need of salvation. He will die and go to hell, and he may protest as hard as he can that there *is* no hell, but he will be right *in it,* and no amount of denial and protesting will bring him out!

We are talking about something very different. Here we are dealing with a principle which God has made concerning words; not the odd, occasional words we speak, but the pattern of words and thoughts we may have used all our lives, which are shaping us and our circumstances, 'making us or breaking us' whether we realise it or not. Our words give away what is in our heart; they are simply the overflow of what my heart is full of.

This is what James meant about the tongue influencing the whole of our body. It is essential to realise this truth when worry attacks us, for our greatest temptation will be to talk constantly about our problems, to speak out our inability and fear, to question God and his purposes.

But how should we conduct ourselves when facing some great need? How should we speak? Suppose your problem is a financial need. Your bank statement shows you are £2,000 'in the red'. Mind over matter would say: 'I don't believe that, it's just not true.' The Christian who knows the power of *his words* and the power of *God's Word* would say: 'Father, you see this need, but your Word says that you are our Shepherd and we should not lack any good thing. I deny poverty and lack the right to rule my life in the Name of Jesus, and thank you Father for supplying this need. You are caring for me.'

Your problem may be an unsaved loved one. You see their life, the way they are carelessly going down the path to Hell and it would be so easy to voice your fears and worries. But the wise Christian says: 'Father, your Word says that we and our house will be saved; that "great will be the peace of our children" for "great peace have they that love thy law". So I thank you that you are working in this situation; by faith I see John/Mary serving you, living a clean life, and the power of the devil broken over them.'

Your problem may be sickness. The pain and symptoms are there but you believe God can heal you. You do not deny that sickness is there, you *deny it the right* to remain in your body, when God has promised us health and wholeness. You deny it the right to destroy

132

you when Jesus healed us 2,000 years ago by his stripes. ('Who his own self bare our sins in his own body on the tree, that we, being dead to sins, should live unto righteousness; by whose stripes you were healed.' 1.Peter 2,24). So you begin to praise God for bringing this healing into manifestation in your body.

You pray for wisdom concerning the doctors, their recommended treatment or diet. God may lead you to have some of these, or may lead you to trust him entirely for your recovery, without medical aid. It is not a question of either/or, but often a case of human and divine help.

Our subject here is not healing. It is a far greater and more complicated subject than can be dealt with in a few sentences. Each person must act as *God* leads them. Each case is different and God has many ways of helping his children. We are not to dictate to others but to humbly support and pray for them, not condemn and criticise.

In every need, whatever the problem, God's principle remains the same; he has given us the responsibility and privilege of choosing to speak creative, faith-filled, loving words, and learning to discard the words of doubt, defeat, fear, worry and criticism. Remember — *your words will make or break you!*

20

Worry or the Word?

Every Christian must sooner or later make the choice
of letting his life and thinking be dominated by *Worry*
or the *Word of God.* Let us compare the results of
worrying or believing God's Word.

Worry does not bring a solution to our problems.
Trust in God's Word points the way out.

Meditating on our problems brings us deeper into
failure.

Meditating in God's Word brings obedience,
prosperity and good success (Joshua 1,8).

Worry has killed thousands, perhaps millions, of
people.

God's Word brings quickening and healing for
spirit, soul and body (Psalm 119,50 and Proverbs
4, 20-22).

Worry has never made anyone glad.

God's Word fills us with joy (Jeremiah 15,16).

Worry causes us to believe fear and the lies of the
devil.

God's Word produces faith and helps us to believe
God (Rom.10,17).

Worry crushes the lonely and drives them to despair.

God's Word and the Living Word — Jesus — has
been sent to heal the brokenhearted and set the
captives free (Luke 4,16-21).

Worry will cause our mind to be clouded with
confusion, so that we cannot see our way clearly.

God's Word will shine upon our path and we shall not stumble (Psalm 119,105).

Worry causes us to be taken up with ourselves and the greatness of our problems.

God's Word will turn our eyes to the One who is far greater and who is worthy of our worship (Psalm 18, 1-3 and 28-30).

Worry will shorten our life.

Long life is promised to those who trust and obey their God and his Word (Psalm 91).

Worry is an intruder which is trying to take up residence in our lives.

God's Word should be ruling in our hearts, leaving us no room for this unwelcome guest (Philippians 4, 6 and 7 and Col.3,16).

Worry makes us concentrate on our problem.

God's Word points us to the solution (Psalm 119,130).

Worry is a negative force.

God's Word is a positive power (Heb.1,3 and John 6,63).

Worry causes us to magnify what the devil is doing.

The Word of God magnifies how *God* is working (Isaiah 55,8-11).

Worry makes us become introvert.

God's Word causes us to look up to him and out to the needs of others (2.Thess.2,15-17).

Worry is a dead-end street.

Obedience to God's Word brings us into a glorious future (Deuteronomy 28, 1-14).

Worry hinders our usefulness for God.

His Word makes us strong and effective (Psalm 1,2-3 and 2 Tim.3,16,17).

Worry is a weapon of Satan used *against us*.

God's Word, the sword of the Spirit will fight *for* us (Hebrews 4,12 and Ephesians 6,17).

Worry will leave us defenceless against the devil's

attacks.

The Word of God will give us discernment and protection (Proverbs 7, 1-5, 24-27).

Worry and fear will defile our thoughts, filling us with condemnation.

God's Word purifies us (Psalm 119,11 and John 15,3).

Worry is negative seed which if sown in the heart will eventually destroy.

God's Word is the positive seed which if sown in good ground, brings forth life and victory (Psalm 126,6 and Matth.13, 2-23).

Worry weighs us down with unhappiness and depression.

Believing God's Word clothes us with a garment of praise (Isaiah 61,3).

Worry does not show us a true picture of our situation.

God's Word acts as a mirror wherein we see things clearly (James 1, 22-25).

Worry is something temporary.

God's Word will stand for ever (Is.40,8 and Matth.24,35).

Worry brings weakness and inability.

The Word of God speaks divine authority and power into our situation (Luke 4, 36 and Matth. 8,8).

Worry brings unrest and stress.

God's Word brings peace (Psalm 119,165).

Worry will bring us to despair.

God's Word offers us a new hope (Psalm 119,49-50 and 147).

Millions of Christians throughout the centuries have proved that using and obeying God's Word instead of allowing worry to dominate their thinking, has completely changed their situation. One good example of this is the story Dr Yonggi Paul Cho tells about one of his church members. (In 1978 I had the thrill of interpreting for Dr Cho at a large conference in Strasbourg. He is the pastor of the world's largest church with over 700,000 members in Seoul, Korea.)

One day, this little lady came to Pastor Cho for prayer. She had cancer and the doctors gave her only a short time to live. He told her to go home and write out ten thousand times, 'By his stripes I am healed', and to read each line through aloud after writing it.

The lady went home and took a large pad of paper. She began to write: 'No. 1 By his stripes I was healed!', then she read it aloud. 'No. 2 By his stripes I was healed' — read it aloud; 'No. 3 By his . . .'

How laborious, how boring it was, hour after hour she sat there writing and reading in turn. But she knew it was a matter of life and death, and she kept at her writing day after day. At the end of a week she was finished and ran to see Pastor Cho. She waved the huge sheet of notes at him, crying:

'I've finished, Pastor! Ten thousand times "By his stripes I am healed".'

'How's your cancer doing?' asked Pastor Cho.

'My cancer? Oh, I forgot all about my cancer. Why, I must be healed!' She shouted for joy — she was indeed healed!

What brought about this healing? Her obedience? Her writing? Mind over matter? God healed her because she was more taken up with his Word than with her problem. She concentrated on the *solution* and not on her *need*. The Word of God began to take root in her heart as never before; it took hold of her; it had first place in her thinking and almost without her knowing it, her faith was growing and taking over where worry and despair had previously held her in its grip.

Our problem may not be cancer or some other illness and God has many ways to bring healing and help to us. He is a God of variety. We are not giving this example as a patent recipe for the healing of cancer.

This is what God led Pastor Cho to tell this lady, and it worked.

The point we are making here is, that this lady found that being immersed and taken up with the Word of God brought greater dividends than worry. She *chose* to do this. She could have said:

'Why, how hard our Pastor is. He didn't even pray for me or sympathise with me. As if I'm not ill enough now and he tells me to write out a Bible verse ten thousand times. I'm not going to do it. No, I'm not going to do it!' But instead of rebelling she followed Pastor Cho's instructions and her obedience was rewarded.

An evangelist was travelling home one night. He drove in the night as it was cooler and his tyres were wearing thin. It was during the days of the 'Great Depression' and he and his young family had known many financial crises. He was returning from an evangelistic campaign, having no further bookings, and as he drove, the devil began to tempt him to worry. Where was the money coming from? They wouldn't have anything to eat. What would his wife say? Who was going to pay the bills?

After a while, it seemed as if he heard the wheels through the open window, singing 'What are you going to do now?' First one wheel; then the second wheel joined in; then the third, until all four sang a quartet — monotonous and threatening. 'What are you going to do now? What are you going to do now? What are you going to do now? What are you going to do *now?*'

But instead of joining in the worry-song of the wheels, the evangelist shouted out: 'What am I going to do *now*? I'll tell you what I'm going to do now; I'm ·going to go home and sleep like a baby, *and act as if God's Word is so.*'

And that is just what he did. The next day, God opened up more meetings for him and he had gained another great victory in 'winning over worry'. He chose to trust what God had promised in his Word, he was not only *able* but *willing* to perform, and that he would do it for the evangelist and his family.

It would do us all good if we were more taken up with God's Word, instead of our worries. Jesus said that even though heaven and earth would pass away, yet his Word would never pass away. What God has spoken echoes on through time and eternity. When he spoke to the universe and started it rolling and functioning, it began and has never stopped yet. It will continue to function until God speaks to stop it in its course. All things in the universe are upheld by the word of God's power. God believes in his Word; he believes in his written Word also, and lays it down as the priority for us as his children to live by.

God said to Joshua: 'This book of the law shall not depart out of your mouth; but you shall meditate therein day and night, that you may observe to do according to all that is written therein; for then you will make your way prosperous, and then you will have good success' (Joshua 1,9). God was giving Joshua a success formula; a victory strategy. Joshua was to remember and obey God's words to him and all Israel. He was to meditate on them and to continually speak them out, as well as obeying them.

When we think of 'meditation' we often imagine an Indian Guru or Buddhist monk sitting cross-legged in silent meditation; or long-haired hippies chanting mantras and invoking the spirits. But meditation came originally from God.

What does it mean, 'to meditate'? Have you ever watched a cow chewing cud? She has four compartments to her stomach and can return grass to her mouth which she swallowed a while before. This is part of her digestive process. God tells us to chew all the goodness out of his Words which we have taken into ourselves. We must think it over, turn it over and over in your mind and heart not superficially, but contemplatively; absorb it into us as we would soak up the rays of the sun; let God's words penetrate through every part of our being.

Meditation also means 'to mutter', 'to repeat quietly'. God wants us to speak out his Word as we go about our daily tasks, and let the energising, cleaning power of the Holy Scriptures be released in us. God's promise was not just for Joshua, it is for *us too! We* will have good success as we follow God's instructions.

I read the true story of a minister who put an advertisement in the local newspaper, asking for people to donate Bibles which they did not need. A man rang up, saying he had a load for him.

The minister visited the man, who was the owner of a public house, and was taken into a back room. Piled up on the table were heaps of new, black Bibles. 'Where did you get them?' the minister asked.

'You saw that church, over the road? All the couples who get married there receive a Bible as a gift from the vicar. After the wedding, they come here for a drink or the reception, and they leave the Bibles here. They don't want something as old-fashioned as a *Bible* in their new home,' the landlord replied, laughing.

The minister gladly took the Bibles — over 70 of them, imagining the joy and hope they would bring Christians behind the Iron Curtain, and thanking God for this answer to prayer. Yet his heart was saddened that these young couples were throwing away the very thing they would need in their life together; the very thing which should guide, support and direct them — the Word of God.

They trusted in their love, their youth and forgot that in every life, sooner or later, love and youth will not be enough to help us face the problems which arise. Human love becomes bankrupt if God is left out and youth will one day become age.

The only things which will not change and lose their worth are eternal values. The house which is not built on the rock of doing the Word of God will fall when the storm comes.

Let's begin to give God's Word its rightful place in our lives. It is our responsibility to use this 'sword of the Spirit' — the Holy Scriptures — in the face of every need and in every situation, instead of giving in to worry, fear and defeat.

'Worry or the Word?' Let us choose 'the Word' every time!

21

Does your Wallet Worry You?

A large proportion of our daily worries are concerned with finances. We are told that in many marriages this is the major cause for divorce. Each of us at some time has known financial pressure and wondered how we would make ends meet, but some people live like that for years, or even all of their lives.

When Helen and I got married I was a junior pastor in Switzerland. We lived with the senior pastor's family and paid for our board and lodging out of the wages the church gave me. There was not a lot left over, and when we left Switzerland to live for a while in England I took a job in a toffee factory. Stirring huge vats of caramel and my white overalls covered in black liquorice mixture did not exactly make us one of 'the idle rich' after paying rent and expenses. The only flat we could afford was shockingly cold and the furniture terrible, but we did not mind very much as we expected to be moving on to God's next step for us very soon; we knew it was only a transitional period.

One day somebody gave me a copy of a book about 'seed-faith'. It spoke about the scriptural principle of sowing and reaping, of giving and receiving. If you need friends, then start to show kindness and love to others and God will let it flow back to you. If you need finances, give as God shows you and see God supply your need. Sow a seed of what you need and expect God to give a harvest back to you.

The farmer always receives a bigger harvest (provided the conditions are right) than the amount of seed he planted. It is a law of nature, and if this was not the case we would probably all have died of starvation long ago. The farmer expects this and nobody would say he was wrong to expect to receive more back than he originally sowed.

We had always given our tithe — a tenth of our income — to God, but had never expected to receive much, if anything, back. We just thought we would get by somehow, but that God was really interested in our finances . . . I determined to try this out, for the book said that in Malachi 3,10 God has challenged us to *prove* him. He said that if we bring all the tithes into his storehouse, he would open the windows of heaven and pour out a blessing upon us so that there would not be room enough to contain it! Strange that we had never noticed that before in this way.

So the next time we gave our tithe, we added some extra money as an offering and sent it to the place God showed us.

We prayed like this: 'Father, we are giving this money as a seed to your work and we pray you will multiply it back to us in our need. If you want us to stay in England, then give us money for a deposit on a house, but if you want us to return to Europe to evangelise (which is what we felt was God's leading), then give us the deposit for a car. (We had never had a car.) Thank you, Father.'

For a while nothing happened, then people started to bring us things we needed, or give us nice clothes; then came the day when a man gave me an envelope and said: 'Here is the deposit for a car and you are to go and evangelise in Europe. . .' The very words we had prayed.

We bought the car, gave up our flat and travelled to Switzerland; our little boy Paul, who was almost three, was wedged in the back seat between cases and boxes, and the rest of our luggage was piled high on the top of the car. After a wedding we were to attend, we had only two weeks of meetings booked, but we knew God was going to open up more. It seemed a crazy thing to do, so illogical, so irresponsible . . . yet it was what God had showed us to do.

The two weeks turned into three months in Switzerland, then a further four months in Germany, Norway, Sweden and Holland. We preached in churches and at house meetings, Bible schools and conferences, just wherever God opened the doors. This was a 'faith' venture, for we had very little in the bank and very few contacts, yet God helped us in a wonderful way. The car payments had to be paid every month and there were repairs and petrol for the car over all the thousands of kilometres we travelled, and boat tickets, etc., etc.

It was no good wondering *how* God was going to help us, for he tested us and provided for us in many different ways. I remember in Sweden a mission had arranged a series of meetings in different towns and provided an interpreter who travelled with us in his own car. We had had several meetings and he never gave us any money. Soon we had hardly any petrol left and no money to buy any more.

Helen became angry and said I should ask him, but I did not like to do it. We sat in stony, seething silence for a long while, staring at the back of his car in front of us, wondering if he was going to give us anything at all, and furious with each other.

Well, of course he *did* give us something and it was a generous offering, but that was a worrying time.

Being a preacher is not the same as any other job. A plumber or carpenter, a garage mechanic or the man who repairs your washing machine will give you a bill for the services rendered to you. His time, materials, travel costs, etc., will all be included, with V.A.T. added on top.

But a preacher cannot do that. Even if he charged a

certain amount for preaching, his time and travelling expenses (which some do) he is unable to estimate the years of experience, the agonising battles in prayer, the searching for answers, the hours of Bible study, the crises he has gone through, the pouring out of himself spiritually, mentally and physically, which enable him to *give you those answers you are looking for,* in his sermon or ministry. These are too costly and impossible to calculate in pounds and pence.

Sometimes people ask: 'How much shall we give you for preaching, Brother?' We always reply: 'That's between you and the Lord. We cannot name any figure.' Whether we receive little or much, if we receive no money at all — not even for travelling expenses — we thank the pastor and leave the matter with the Lord. It is not easy to do that when you need the money, sometimes desperately. 'Wallet-worry' begins hammering at the door of your mind and heart, insisting to come in.

It is easy to get bitter when your payment for preaching is a box of chocolates and a record from the book table, and what do you tell the missionary for whom you've been interpreting when the offering for him and yourself as the interpreter is DM22.50 (£7.50)?

One pastor said to me: 'Brother, I'm living by faith like you!' I could not reply for I knew he owned his own business and was paid expenses by his church, his wife had a full-time job, they had no children and they lived in his family's house and paid no rent! 'By faith', indeed!

I did not begrudge this pastor his good fortune, but what did hurt was the careless, almost sarcastic way he spoke concerning something he knew nothing about.

We have shared with you some other illustrations of financial squeezes we have had and how God has helped us out. There are always two sides to the coin, two sides to every answer and to every miracle in our life. There is the human side, the conditions we must fulfil to receive, and the divine side of God's intervention.

These conditions could be faith, love, giving, integrity, prayer, obedience to God's Word and leading, refusing to worry and be bitter if things did not turn out as we had hoped, an open heart, living an honest, clean life . . . and many other things we could name which will bring God's blessings upon us.

God does not hold out a magic formula, which, when used, provides the answer every time. He has certain principles in his Word and if we will make these our *life-style* (not just do them now and again), we will create a climate for a harvest of blessing to come upon us.

You may have a good job, be able to pay your bills, have put by quite a bit 'for a rainy day', and are tolerably satisfied with your financial situation. But with inflation and rocketing prices, firms going bankrupt on every hand, millions out of work and more to follow, then 'wallet-worry' comes knocking at the door of countless hearts today.

Being an evangelist and Bible teacher living 'by faith', this is one of the areas in which we have been most tested. This is something for which we are trying to find answers, to help ourselves and countless others who suffer and lack. We shared this principle of giving and how it worked for us in 1970 and many times since, but there have been other times when we did not receive what we had believed for and could not understand why. Later we saw that perhaps the project was right but not the timing.

At another time perhaps there was some other reason, but we know that it is not God's fault, it is always *ours. We* are the ones who do not always know *how to receive* from our Father. Then there are the occasions when he literally pours out his blessings and showers us with his goodness, and we feel ashamed for not trusting more.

146

What is God's attitude to our finances? Is he blind or heedless to the fact that the state of our wallet or bank account worries us? It seems that many of us Christians are very hypocritical about money. We seldom mention money in church, except to condemn it as 'the root of all evil' and the 'ungodly unrighteous mammon', and take the attitude that we are 'spiritual' if we can hardly pay our bills and our car breaks down every other week.

Yet the very same people join the strike for more pay, are constantly complaining how dear everything is, and are bitter against those who seem to be doing better financially.

It seems as though we have swallowed the lie that *God* wants us *poor*, just about scraping through, barely getting along, and the *devil* is the one who is offering us money, luxury and abundance if we follow the thinking and ways of the world. We are caught between the two, not wanting to go against God's will, yet our hearts are hankering after enough and some to spare.

Preachers preach about Jesus not having a place to lay his head and how his disciples gave up their source of financial income to follow him, and Peter and John had 'no silver or gold' to give to the beggar at the temple gate. We read how hard it is for a rich man to enter the Kingdom of Heaven, overlooking that Jesus really was saying how hard it is for those *'who trust in riches'* to enter the kingdom.

But let us examine this more closely. Was Jesus really *so* poor? He was born in a stable and into a humble family. Yet Joseph his father had his own carpentry business. We do not read that Jesus went without food and clothes, a house to live in and the normal necessities of life. His robe was so unusual or beautiful, that the Roman soldiers at the cross gambled for it.

Jesus worked until he was 30 years old at the carpenter's bench and probably earned a good living. When he entered into the three years of his ministry and became a wandering preacher, the impression is not given that he slept under the hedge every night and became an ascetic who thought it more 'spiritual' to fast and suffer hunger than to eat.

On the contrary; he was often invited to feasts and dinner parties; he sometimes stayed in the homes of friends and enjoyed their hospitality. Some even called him a 'man gluttonous and a wine-bibber', because he ate and drank normally and did not fast as often as John the Baptist (Matth.11,19).

Jesus did not condemn the woman who poured rich, expensive spikenard over him, though the hypocrites said it could have been given to the poor.

Rich men and women gave alms to him and his disciples, even women from Herod's household. Imagine Jesus and his disciples walking through the towns and villages, followed by a group of women who had been healed and who, perhaps, helped on the 'domestic side' for this evangelistic party: they took some feeding and caring for!

The Apostle Paul several years later, on his missionary journeys, sometimes travelled with a group. They needed food, clothes, boat tickets and were well enough provided for that they could take gifts of money from the Church to those in need, and were not themselves counted among the needy. Paul's tent making must have helped sometimes, but being a travelling missionary left little time for a private business.

When they needed to pay the taxes, Jesus provided the money through the miracle in the mouth of the fish.

He provided an abundance of food on two occasions for thousands of people in the desert, and was concerned lest they be faint and weary from hunger. A rich man provided a tomb for him, and at the cross Jesus found a place for his mother Mary to live and be cared for when he was no longer there, by giving her over to John, who 'took her to his own house'.

Jesus knew that living on this earth we have certain needs and he delighted to help people.

The Bible says: '. . . our Lord Jesus Christ, that, though he was rich, yet for your sakes he became poor, that you through his poverty might be rich.' This means spiritual and financial lack should be done away with, for want and poverty were part of the curse of the law (Deuteronomy 28), and Jesus came to break the curse of the law on the cross of Calvary (Galatians 3,13).

The word 'rich' means *to have enough for yourself* **and** *an overflow to help others in their need.* God is concerned about our wallet and our financial struggles. He wants us to give this part of our life — our finances — over to his lordship and find out his will for us in this area. Some people are only saved as far as their wallets!

A man was stepping into the water to be baptised, when his pastor said: 'Hey Jack, hang on, you've still got your wallet in your pocket.'

'Yes, I know, Pastor,' Jack replied, 'but my wallet needs baptising too!'

Water baptism for believers is a symbol of going down into death and coming up to newness of life, and Jack saw that the money side of his life needed changing and purifying. He wanted God to bless his money and help him to use it to spread the Gospel, instead of it being squandered or spent unwisely.

Jack had realised something which many of us have not, namely that the way we think about money, the way we spend it, our lifestyle and everything connected with our finances needs to be brought to the cross of Jesus.

Our money, the financial side of our life, our credits and debits, our abundance and lack should all be given over to God. So often we look upon money as 'mammon', something worldly, unspiritual and definitely not a thing we would ask God about. But money is

149

necessary for our daily living and we need to find out God's way of obtaining and using it.

God wants us to learn not to misuse money or to make it our goal in life. However, he *is not against us having money, but against money having us!*

Money is neutral — neither good nor bad — it depends how we use it. The Bible did not say it is the root of all evil, but that 'the *love* of money is the root of all evil'. The same money which is used to gamble could feed thousands of starving people. The same money which is used to print pornographic literature could be used to print evangelistic material and Bibles.

Money is neutral; so are several other things. Water, which is one of the necessities of life, can bring devastation, flooding and death. A car brings me from A to B, but in the hands of a reckless, drunken driver is a death trap.

No, money is not something evil, something 'worldly', that God turns away from in disgust and leaves us to struggle on as best we can on our own, because he cannot or will not help us in our finances. He is very concerned about the state of our wallet and bank account, and wants to help us.

Church tradition has taught that being poor is a good state for us to be in, that then we would be humble, and the temptations which riches bring would not touch us. In one way this is true, yet we all know people who have very little and if offered more, they would be too proud to take it. You can be proud with 20 pence in your pocket! Yet there are others who often suffer want but would share their last bite with someone in need, and their hearts are full of love. It depends on the attitude of our heart, and it is dangerous to generalise.

I know people who have much of this world's goods and *are* proud and stingy, but I know others who are simple, natural and always willing to give. Some have given many thousands of pounds, millions of dollars to spread the Gospel and to help others.

The Old Testament gives us many examples of God blessing his servants, Abraham, Isaac, Jacob, Joseph, Job and many others, and making them wealthy. When Solomon asked God for wisdom, he gave him wealth as a bonus.

There are Christian communities where everybody pools their belongings, even selling their houses and giving the money into a general fund. We are told that because the 'Early Church' did this, we should do the same.

However, that is only half the truth. When the Christians did this 'and had all things in common', they did it to help those who were in genuine need. There was no social system, no government help, and this was one way they used to help the situation. There were also widows and orphans to feed.

Yet not everybody sold their house, gave up their home and joined in to make one 'happy family'. When Ananias and Sapphira sold their land, and lied to Peter and the Holy Ghost about the price, Peter said to them: 'Why have you done this? You could have kept some of the money. You were at liberty to do so, but why lie about it?' (Acts 5, 1-4).

If we do not realise that God is *for* us, not *against* us in the financial side of our life, then *these questions, this uncertainty will block our trust in God to help us come out of our 'wallet-worries'.*

If we have the feeling that every Christian should really take the 'poverty vow' but they are not spiritual enough, how can we help others and also give to evangelise the world before Jesus comes?

While not wanting to heap riches and wealth upon ourselves, to squander money and be selfish and blind to the needs of others, let us not believe that those who are suffering want are nearer to God than those living in the 'rich capitalistic West'. This impression is often given in Christian circles nowadays.

Slogans like: 'Better to die than live to be a consumer' are *not scriptural,* they are *political propaganda.* Have you ever been to the countries where they are promoted? If so, you cannot believe this lie.

God will supply all of our need, not according to our old-age pension, not according to our wage packet, but according to his riches in glory, by Christ Jesus! This promise was given to those Christians who had been giving liberally, not always out of their abundance, but also out of their lack, like the widow with her two mites.

Get God's wisdom, God's way to solve your wallet-worries; be convinced that it is his will for you to come out of debt, to have enough for yourself and to spare for others.

Spurgeon used to laugh about a fish swimming in the ocean worrying that one day there would not be enough water for him! We are just as stupid when we worry instead of trusting our Father, to dispel all of our 'wallet-worries'.

I do not need to know how many miles of cable and thousands of screws there are in an aeroplane before I will board it; I just need to get in and fly to my destination, leaving the cables and screws to the aeroplane manufacturer. It is *his* business to worry about that.

In the same way I do not need to know *how* God will do it, but just that he *will* do it, for he is faithful who has promised!

22

Thoughts at New Year

When the new year lies before us like an unwritten page and the unknown future has not yet revealed the experiences it holds, then our thoughts turn automatically back to the old year. Like somebody who discovers long-lost treasures in a drawer, examines them lovingly and rereads precious letters, so the miracle of memory enables us to relive and re-experience the past.

Light and shadows, joy and pain, hope and despair, sickness and health — these contrary twins run through the life of every person. Reaching a desired goal gives us joy, new strength and fulfilment but very often we seem to drag ourselves through each day. We are like a twig tossed here and there on the water. We feel helpless when the waves of problems, sickness and anxiety rage against us.

We form new attachments but other old relationships and friendships are broken off. How many marriages were dissolved last year because men and women are driven by a restless, egoistic passion to go their own way and satisfy their every personal whim, not concerned if their partner is hurt or their childrens' lives destroyed?

Sometimes we are overwhelmed by the thought: 'Is there *nobody* to help us? Is God really interested in us *personally*? *Can* he — and still more important — *will* he help me? Millions of people are facing the new year alone. They dread the thought of another *day* alone, and when they think of a whole year, they panic or fall into deep depression. The one they loved and trusted has betrayed them, or left them through death, and the pain is unbearable, stabbing like a hundred knives in their heart.

I once read these words which were written by an unknown author: 'One night I had a dream. I was walking with the Lord, my God, along the seashore. Scenes from my life passed before my eyes and by every picture I discovered footprints in the sand. Sometimes I saw two sets of footprints, then again only one pair. This confused me, for I observed that every time I was troubled with fear, anxiety or a sense of defeat, only *one* set of footprints was to be seen. So I turned to the Lord and said: "You have promised me, Lord Jesus, you would always walk with me, if I would follow you. But I have just made the discovery that in the most difficult experiences of my life, only one set of footprints was in the sand. When I needed you the most, why weren't you there to help me?"

'Then my Lord answered me: "Those times when you only saw *one set* of footprints in the sand, I was always *carrying* you".'

How beautiful is the picture that God is helping us through the storms in our lives even when we do not realise it. How often have his angels saved us from certain death and we have praised our own ingenuity and laughed at the thought that he had helped us. God draws us to him in countless situations, in order that he might walk with us through our lives and uphold us. But he is a 'gentleman' and will not force his way in. He never forces his presence and fellowship on us. He calls lovingly to us and offers us eternal life and assistance in our needs.

Jesus also spoke of this picture when he came, as God's Son, to this earth. He called himself the Good Shepherd who cares for his sheep. We can imagine how he carries the weak, tired lambs on his shoulder, exactly the same as he wants to carry *us* through the difficult, apparently hopeless situations in life.

Are we trusting in our intelligence, education or experience as the only supports to accompany us into this new year? Are we trusting in relatives, friends or some philosophy of life to carry us through? Humanism would like to teach us that man is good and wise, that he can build his own future, that he needs no God because he is his own saviour. Humanism would lie to us that the world is getting better and would try to confuse us spiritually.

But we must not let ourselves be deceived. Civilised, educated and intelligent as we are, often self-righteous and proud of our abilities and achievements, nevertheless we are still not able to overcome fear, anger, jealousy and the countless other negative tendencies in our nature. We hide these things and show a smiling face to the world but only God and we ourselves know what our heart really looks like. Jesus does not come to condemn us and point an accusing finger at us. He comes with love and forgiveness. At this time of the year it is good to take a spiritual inventory and clear out of our lives what should not be there, and order new stocks of patience, forgiveness and faith, as necessary.

The new year will contain wonderful hours of blessing and happiness, but there will also be times of uncertainty and danger. We have never been this way before, therefore we need someone to guide us who has already walked on this path — Jesus Christ, the Son of the living God. His help will not come automatically to us, we must ask him for it and trust his love every hour of the day in this new year.

Place every worry and care unreservedly in his hands and know that he is walking *with* you, living *in* you, and carrying you through every crisis. For as the old hymn says, that hand 'holds the key of all unknown . . .' and our hand too.

LIVE IN THE NOW!

I do not need to know the future
That lies before me,
Or the details far ahead;
I just need to know the next step
That I must take —
The next thing that waits to be done.
The unborn years that beckon in the distance
Are not mine to approach today.
I was created to live in the now
Not in the future or yesterday.
The knowledge of what tomorrow holds
Would be burdensome for me;
And if through impatience, fear or curiosity
I seek to discover it,
I shall only be marred.
As the sand falls a grain at a time in the glass
So will I live my life
With its millions of seconds in a year —
Steadily . . . one at a time.
As the car headlights beam on the road
Showing the next few feet,
So will the lamp of his Word light my path,
Cheering, directing, warning of the danger.
Finding his plan and will, and laying down ambition,
I will pray, work and do the best that I can,
Trusting, as he lives his life — through me.

The above poem was written by Helen. I gave her
some ideas towards it.

Taking this attitude will banish care and worry, fear
of the future, and enable us to set our face with joy and
anticipation in that direction.

Sometimes I compare the old year with Moses, and
the new year with Joshua. In Joshua 1, we read: '. . .
the Lord spoke unto Joshua the son of Nun, Moses'
minister, saying: "Moses my servant is dead; now

therefore arise, go over this Jordan . . .".' Moses, like the old year, had his chance. Now comes Joshua, and it's his turn. I can imagine the Children of Israel saying:

'Why are you doing this, Joshua? Moses never did it this way. You must do things as Moses did.'

But Joshua knew that he must make his own way, as God led *him*. God is a God of variety and is not lost for ways and means to reveal himself to his people. Joshua may not have called down the plagues upon Egypt, led the Israelites across the dry 'Red Sea' seabed and received the Ten Commandments written with the finger of God on the tablets of stone, as Moses did, but it was *Joshua* who called the sun to stand still in his tracks and *Joshua* who finally took God's people into Canaan — even Moses, because of disobedience, never finally got in.

So give the new year a chance in its own right. What you expected and did not see materialise in the old year 'Moses', may come to pass in 'Joshua'. Look forward with expectation instead of looking backward, worrying and fretting.

A car has four gears to help it go forward and only *one* to go backwards. We should go forwards four times as quickly, as backwards! Put your faith and energy into 'gears' which will help you to go on, and spend as little time as possible in attempting to go back. Historians tell us that Alexander the Great wept when he saw that there was nothing more for him to achieve. He was driven by a passion to conquer but when his goals were reached, his life became empty. With God there are always new worlds to conquer, but we must begin by putting the past behind us and reaching out and stepping into new things of the future.

A young man sat in a meadow where the farmer had just mown the grass. It was a favourite place for him, and the previous day he had watched the butterflies sucking nectar and hovering over the flowers. Sure enough, on this day too, a butterfly came and settled on some of the flowers. But there was no more nectar, the flowers were cut down and dead.

The man wondered what the butterfly would do. Would it stay there because it had found something yesterday? Would it fly around and fret and worry at not finding anything today? That is what we would have done perhaps — living in the past, squeezing the lemon that is already bone dry!

But the butterfly had more sense than that. It spread out its wings and flew away to another field which was full of flowers just waiting for it to come and take of their spoils. The man smiled, got up from the grass where he had been sitting, and squaring his shoulders, put his own disappointment behind him and walked into a future full of opportunity!

23

From Resignation to Motivation

Some people are past the worrying stage and have given in to resignation. What does resignation mean? When somebody is in a state of resignation, he is passive, he has reached a dead-end street in life; he makes no progress, shows no growth and is in a state of depression. When he speaks he says something like this: 'Things will never get any better. It's not worth trying. I'm not worth anything anyway. I will never achieve or amount to anything. I've resigned myself to the situation. God cannot use me, etc., etc.'

There are many reasons why a person can get in this condition — disappointment, fear, bitterness, lack of opportunity to develop, boredom, unbelief, worry, sickness, depression, inferiority complex, and perhaps many other things. Not only can individuals reach this point but whole families and even a church.

Resignation is a negative condition and produces nothing positive. Most of us have lived perhaps for a while on 'Resignation Avenue' but some people have lived there for many years!

On this street everything is very still and lifeless. The houses look old and dark, paint is flaking off the doors and the windows. The gardens are overgrown with weeds and there is little or only tasteless fruit on the fruit trees. The people who live here live only in the memories of the past. In fact, they are not living, they are only vegetating.

But there is another street and it's called 'Motivation

Boulevard'. Here the houses and buildings are freshly painted and designed in many different ways, for their owners are always open to new ideas. Many cars and lorries piled high with excellent wares are making their way along the street. Stimulating conversation and discussions can be heard; there is music and laughter, and enthusiasm can be felt in the air.

The people are energetic and waste no time with worrying and regret. Instead they discuss and consider how they can do things even better or avoid making the same mistakes again. The gardens of the houses are a sight to see, filled with the most beautiful flowers and vegetation, and the branches of the fruit trees are bowed down beneath the weight of their marvellous fruit.

Life never dies out on 'Motivation Boulevard'. This street runs in the direction of the future.

And what about us? What street are we living on? On which street would God like us to live? That's easy to see.

If worry and resignation cause us to think and act negatively, then they can never come from God. He is a God full of creativity, activity, variety, colour; a God of progress, of making anew, the God of a new beginning. Nature — his handiwork — is full of life, and this life pulsates on through every created being or thing in the universe. God has *never* worried, *never* given in to resignation, or he would have given us up long ago.

How does motivation actually function? A person can be motivated to good or bad. Let's consider being motivated to do something 'good'.

When God made Creation, he had an *inner picture* of every animal and every flower within himself. He saw the rose, heard the bird song before it was even created.

When he created Adam and Eve, they satisfied the *desire* or longing of his heart to have somebody who would voluntarily love and obey him.

160

This 'seeing' and 'desiring' inspired and motivated God to create these things. Motivation causes us to go into action to accomplish or express something. Even as God was motivated to create through this *inner picture* and *inner desire,* we too, can use this faculty of imagination of mind and spirit which he has passed on to us, to bring us out of worry and resignation, to victory and motivation.

Take off the 'spectacles' you have been wearing for so long. Through these spectacles you have only seen your limitations, your difficulties, your lack of ability and defeat. Let the Word of God bring a new picture of victory, a divine answer to your problem into your heart and before your spiritual eyes.

Use your imagination to paint pictures of God's intervention rather than the devil's destruction. Receive a new vision from God. We need this for in Proverbs 29,18 we read: 'Where there is *no* vision, the people perish or are destroyed, are in a state of resignation.' Begin to see yourself as *God* sees you — through Jesus!

When God sent Jesus, he was motivated by *our need.* We could not save ourselves, and his love moved him to help us. These same three principles can work also in our lives to bring us to motivation, if we happen to be still living on 'Resignation Avenue'. Let's apply them to the situation we are in today.

1. *The new vision*

Perhaps in our Christian walk or in our service for Jesus we have experienced disappointment or frustration. At first we were angry and wanted to hit back, but now we have entered the stage where we sit resigned and passive, our hands folded in our lap, in our corner of self-pity. We live and dream of past victories and the days when God was able to use us — but now?

God says to you: Stand up. Tell that inner man to rise up. Receive a new vision! God hasn't finished with

161

you yet! He has not cast you aside. When Elijah was laying under the juniper tree wishing he could die, God gave him *a new assignment*. He placed or spoke a new picture in Elijah's heart. The *Word of God* will give us a new picture, a new vision.

As Moses lay on his face before God by the Red Sea and all the Children of Israel were crying out that Pharaoh and his army were going to kill them, God said to him: 'Why are you crying unto me? . . . *Get up!* Lift up your rod and stretch it out over the sea, Moses. Receive a new vision in your heart — see the waves rolling back and making a way for you to go through. Throw away the old picture of despair and death.

2. Our next principle was the *inward wish* or *burning desire*. The desire or goal of a sportsman or athlete to be No.1 motivates him to put everything else on one side. He trains and tortures his body until it obeys him and until his performance increases. The burning desire and the inner mental picture where he sees himself winning a gold medal at the Olympics motivates him to continually push forward and not give up until he has reached his goal.

What dreams and desires has God placed in your heart? Perhaps you have shut them away in a cupboard and hidden the key, because you think you can never accomplish the task; or out of disappointment because it has taken so long for your dream to become a reality. You are worried that you have missed God's will for your life. Take these desires and dreams out of the cupboard again; put them under God's searchlight. Let the Holy Spirit show you how you can work together with him, in order that these dreams become a reality.

3. The third reason for motivation was to see and fulfil a *need*. A child is drowning and a man jumps into the water to save it. People are motivated to donate

money; they see the plight of survivors after a catastrophe. We are motivated to help someone because we see their need. In other words, love and compassion move and drive us to do something to alleviate or put an end to the need. In 2 Cor.5,14 the Apostle Paul writes: 'The love of Christ constrains us . . .' (Bruns translation: *'The love of Christ is the essential driving force of our life . . .'*).

To really come out of a state of resignation to motivation, we need fresh impulses, a fresh 'vision', but we also need faith, patience and determination.

Motivation is more than enthusiasm. It is another dimension and power. Enthusiasm for a certain thing is good, it is infectious. Others will catch on and, to a certain degree, you may be able to motivate yourself and them by your enthusiasm.

But *motivation* is much *deeper* than enthusiasm. When you are motivated with God's Word, quickened by his Spirit and walking in step with him, your motivation will not be dependent on other people's opinions. Enthusiasm does not last long if nobody else joins in. If nobody is interested, the whole thing fizzles out very soon. But God-given motivation will carry you through all the obstacles standing in your path. Enthusiasm may last as long as the circumstances are favourable, but will wane after a while, unless it has a more solid foundation.

Jesus' ministry lasted for the brief period of approximately three years. The first year is known as 'The Year of Inauguration', where Jesus is doing his first miracles and starting to show himself to the world. The second year is 'The Year of Popularity' where the crowds flock around him, and many miracles and great things take place. The people want to make him King and it seems as though nothing can go wrong.

But the third year is 'The year of Opposition'. Here miracles, much teaching and many interesting events are recorded, but the rumble of voices against Jesus

163

makes itself heard, swelling louder until it breaks out into open betrayal and rejection. Jesus is crucified.

If we had been Jesus, during those first two years, it might have been possible for us to be carried along by the enthusiasm of the crowd and the popularity, as was the case with the disciples. They were swept along with the stream, puffed up with pride at being a disciple of this great Teacher, and riding on the balloon of enthusiasm.

But would it have been possible to go through the third year to suffer torture and death on mere 'enthusiasm'? Impossible. It went far deeper — Jesus was motivated by the *inner picture* he had of a lost humanity and himself as the Lamb of God, taking away their sin. He was motivated by a *burning desire* to reconcile us with God, and to do the Father's Will. He was motivated by compassion and *love* and through seeing our *need* — the greatest producers of true motivation.

Later the disciples received true motivation and fleshly enthusiasm dropped off. After they had been stripped of all sham, seen their cowardice and weakness during Jesus' crucifixion and been brought face to face with what it really meant to be his disciple; after they had accepted his forgiveness, taken *his* power — the power of the Holy Spirit — instead of their own, then they went out to change the world, with a deep, unswerving motivation which nothing could turn aside.

After Calvary, they took up residence in 'Resignation Avenue' — all seemed lost. But after the resurrection and the infilling of God's Spirit, they moved, once and for all, onto 'Motivation Boulevard'. How about joining them!

24

Forgiving is Good for You

The Christian life begins with *forgiveness*. This all-important decision when we ask Jesus to forgive us our sins brings us into a new life that is run by spiritual laws or principles, one of which is the need to forgive.

We must continually learn to forgive, and this process continues until we are with the Lord. As long as there are people on the earth and they often make mistakes, we shall have the opportunity to practise forgiveness. As the old proverb says: *'To err is human; to forgive is divine.'*

Forgiving is not easy. Sometimes the most difficult words to say are 'I am sorry'. Many people find it impossible to apologise.

It is easier to forgive someone when they come to us and ask for forgiveness. But, Jesus says that we must even go to the one who holds something against us. Why should we do this? We may be in the right and this person should come and apologise to *us!* We sometimes find many excuses to justify our actions.

As I was interpreting for Brother David du Plessis a few years ago in Switzerland, I saw once again what a great part forgiveness plays in our lives. Forgiveness was a characteristic of David du Plessis' life. When he began his ministry, the Lord said to him: 'If you cannot forgive, then I cannot use you. Don't ever pray the Lord's Prayer, until you have learned to forgive.' I have seen some of the reconciliation ministry between churches and denominations which Brother David practised, and I can really say that without *forgiveness*, this type of ministry would have been *impossible*. One is so often misunderstood, one is so often attacked and wrongfully accused of doing this or that, or words are put into one's mouth which one has never said. David du Plessis had to learn to forgive and because of this attitude of forgiveness, the Lord was able to use him in this important work.

We have no choice, as far as forgiveness is concerned. Either we forgive and Jesus forgives us: *or* we don't forgive and we don't receive his forgiveness. God will not accept any excuse or false pretext when we refuse to practise forgiveness.

Pride is often a hindrance to forgiving. What will other people say if I ask somebody to forgive me? What would happen if he did not accept my apology? But Jesus simply says that *we* are to do the forgiving and then leave the results to him.

We must forgive — even when we don't feel like doing it! Sooner or later in our Christian walk, we make the discovery that our feelings are often more of a hindrance than a help. Our faith must function independently of our feelings. Also in forgivenesss, we must take the first step without waiting for our feelings. We must forgive, whether we find the person likeable or unlikeable. We must also forgive although our five senses want to prove the opposite to us. Most important of all, God wants to see our readiness to forgive. 'Lord, make me willing to forgive . . .' is a good beginning if we feel we have not yet come to the point of full forgiveness.

We should not only forgive, but we should *bless* the person who has wronged us and wish them well. Even if our prayer seems cold and lifeless at the first, after a time, however, we shall be able to pray with conviction and from our heart. The Holy Spirit is very often unable to work as he would like to in our services, because *forgiveness is lacking!*

In Mark 11, 25 Jesus said: 'And when you stand praying, forgive, if you have anything against anyone; that your Father also which is in heaven may forgive you your trespasses.'

Jesus puts prayer and forgiveness very close together here in this passage of scripture. It looks as if the answering of the prayer is dependent on the forgiveness of our heart. Very often we do not realise this fact and we begin to doubt God's willingness to help us if the answer does not come. The problem is more on our side because we do not know or have not fulfilled the conditions — not that God is unwilling to help us.

Medical science tells us that a large percentage of all cancer and arthritic cases are a direct result of unforgiveness and resentment. This shows that they are more knowledgeable in this area than many preachers and Christians. We often think that somebody only needs to go forward for prayer and laying-on of hands and everything will be all right. But when it does not seem to 'work' we conclude that the sick person had no faith or a weak faith which could not help him, or perhaps that the pastor or evangelist who prayed for him had no faith. But this is not always the case. There can be another reason why healing has not come. *The sick person must forgive* in order to obtain or maintain his healing. Resentment was perhaps the cause of the illness and *only by forgiving* can the healing power of God be released in that life.

Very often the sick person is not willing to talk about this question. When asked if he has anybody to forgive, he will loudly say: 'No!' But if the question is presented in another way: 'Has somebody hurt you or done something against you?' then he lets out a stream of grievances, and his words prove that he has not fully forgiven.

Harold Hill told of the case of a woman who was healed of cancer. Later, she became ill again, and the prayer group asked the Lord why this should be. The answer came: 'She hates her daughter-in-law!' When confronted with this, the woman said: 'I would rather die than forgive her!', and she did die, shortly after. How quickly the problems in our churches and families would be solved or not even arise, if we lived a life of forgiveness!

In 1 Cor.11,29 and 30 we read that many Christians have become weak, ill or even died a premature death because they have taken Holy Communion in the wrong attitude — 'not discerning the Lord's body'. One way of 'not discerning the Lord's body' is to hold grudges and bitterness against our brothers and sisters in Christ, who are part of 'the Lord's body'. Instead of being healed and blessed by the act of 'breaking bread', they have 'eaten and drunk damnation to themselves'.

We are unable to measure the terrific consequences of deliberately disobeying this and other words of Scripture. Forgive your marriage partner and children. Forgive pastors and denominations. Help to bring healing to the broken Body of Christ. *Forgive yourself!* Do not live in torment and regret for past mistakes. *God not only forgives but he forgets.*

Some people say: I forgave you for doing such and such a thing, but I'm just reminding you of it. *God is not like that.* His forgiveness is unconditional if we have turned our back on sin and wrongdoing. He has also broken the power of sin over our life, so that we are no longer dominated by it. Therefore march forward in his righteousness and *forgive yourself!*

One 'person' you should not forgive is the devil! Don't get soft towards him and his wiles. We are not to play around with him or have discussions with him, as Eve did, but we are clearly told in James, 4,7 to 'submit yourselves therefore to God. *Resist the devil,* and he will flee from you'.

You may be saying: that's all very well but what has forgiveness to do with worry? The two are closely connected.

If I cannot forgive someone, my mind and emotions are holding on to the hurt or wrong which has been done to me. I relive the harsh words, I relive the traumatic scenes a thousand times in my thoughts.

Bitterness and anger surge through me and build up through the years; they spring up every time that person's name is mentioned, and every time I happen to think of them.

It depends, of course, what the situation is, but many problems may have arisen because of what has happened. The more I hold unforgiveness in my heart, the more I think about these problems and worry rises within me.

On the other hand, the more I worry about something, the more bitter I become that this person could have brought such a need into my life. So worry and unforgiveness are closely connected.

When we *forgive*, we inwardly *let go* of the situation and turn it over to God to deal with, then our worry decreases or ceases altogether. Tension evaporates and peace comes into us; grief is laid aside and God's comfort comes to heal us.

Forgiving is not something which we do occasionally; it should be a *life-style*. Probably every day we have opportunities to hold grudges or to forgive; to store in our memory harsh words and mistakes which others have spoken or committed to be brought out at an appropriate moment and used against them. We also have the opportunity to put these things behind us and forgive as we have been forgiven.

The ability to forgive is not a quality we are born with. It is not a gift we receive when we get saved — it is something we must *learn*. It is also an act of *obedience* to the commands in the Bible to forgive.

The need to *forgive and forget* comes to people of all ages and all walks of life, but when we are young and have a lot to do we do not tend to think or reminisce as much as older people. This is because people getting on in years cannot be as active as before so they tend to live in the past. Their limbs may not be so nimble and the hours seem long to fill every day, so their minds become even more active in reliving past experiences.

While Grandpa talks about the 'good old days', relives his successes and the highlights of his life, Grandma may lapse into depression and remember the painful experiences, the dangers and failures in her past. A person's nature, their state of mind and health and their outlook on life will determine whether they live in the sunshine or shadow of their past.

My grandmother often used to tell me how, years before, Grandfather tried to kill her with an axe. But just before he was able to do so, a strange man came to the door. It was out in the country and very few strangers passed by. He arrived suddenly and disappeared as suddenly, but by the time he had gone, the moment of danger had passed.

This terror-filled night was still fresh in her memory and she relived it again and again, yet the Bible verses she read a few moments before, she was unable to recall. Perhaps the threatened attack was so clear in her mind because she had never really forgiven him.

We may not have someone try to murder us, yet words which are spoken in anger can bruise and tear us apart.

There are countless situations in families which are difficult to forgive: The unfaithfulness of a mate and the anguish of broken dreams and a marriage; the horror and fear which fills the heart of the incest victim as she lies huddled under the bedcovers, terrified lest father or brother come again that night — and the hate which consumes her; the poverty brought about by an alcoholic or drug addict and the helpless rage and frustration which some family members feel; anger against the businessman who cheated you and the church members who slandered you; the children who have turned against everything you taught them and gone their own way.

A man once said to me: 'Brother George, my wife and I have been married 50 years and we've never had a cross word!' I looked at him disbelievingly shaking my head. 'Brother, you are too good for this earth,' I said. 'You should be in heaven already.'

I don't know whether this man had a bad memory, or if he was lying, or if both he and his wife were stupid, or if one partner was so afraid of the other that they did not dare express a different opinion! It is a fact that it is impossible to live 50 years and never disagree, even in the most harmonious marriages.

Marriage is probably the best school in which to learn forgiveness. It is the closest earthly relationship, a picture of Christ and the Church.

The Bible tells us to forgive *quickly*, not to wait six years. It says: 'If you are angry, do not sin. Don't let the sun go down upon your wrath' (Ephesians 4,26). In other words, repent of your anger and ask forgiveness before nightfall. Don't let the situation rankle in your heart allowing it to drag on day after day.

Have you ever gone to bed after a disagreement or quarrel, without putting things right? Susie goes over to her side of the bed, clinging on to the mattress so that she doesn't roll back to the middle and come in contact with Tom.

Tom is on *his* side of the bed, wrapped in a shroud of gloom and sulkiness, wanting to get as far away from Susie as possible. He can't imagine why she made such a fuss. Whatever induced him to marry such a fire-brand!

Susie is seething like a boiling pot, and when he sulks it is even more frustrating as there is nobody to shout back at her!

They toss around on their pillows and eventually fall into a restless sleep. But in the night, Susie wakes up. She and Tom have rolled together in the middle of the bed. His arm is thrown over her and her head is resting

171

on his shoulder. At first she lays still, willing herself to sleep again, but then consciousness floods back and she remembers their quarrel.

Zip! She's over to her side of the bed, kicking out at him with her heel to get out of the way! Anger rises in her again . . . The next morning they get up, each in a terrible mood. Susie's head aches and she longs to cry, but why give that shirker the opportunity to see she's upset? So, with a toss of her head she goes about her work, pushing down the anger and hurt inside.

Tom, who has a different nature, wants to give Susie a different kind of treatment. He won't shout and fuss and lower his dignity as *she* did last night. He won't say harsh words, in fact, he won't say *anything*. This is known as 'the silent treatment'. Tom wants to punish Susie by simply ignoring her, by not acknowledging her presence. He feels smug and self-righteous shut up in his cocoon of sulkiness and silence; *he'll* show her who's the boss in this house!

Tom and Susie are typical of each of us at sometimes, until we learn God's better way, the way of communicating with each other, talking out the problems, praying together — and *forgiving*. If we are going to forgive and make up sometime, why not do it sooner instead of prolonging our misery?

Forgiving is not satisfactory when we are consumed by anger. It is far more satisfying to relive the quarrel, to nurse and pet our grievances and tell ourselves how badly we have been treated. But God's way is better and the sooner we learn this, the richer our lives will become and the less we will have to *worry* about. When we allow God to have the control he begins to straighten out things which have caused the problems in the first place. We have learnt this in our marriage and are *still* learning it, for each day brings new forgiveness challenges.

In the ministry, also, we have many chances to forgive. Sometimes even, family and close friends will misunderstand you. God's leading in each of our lives is so personal that if you are expecting you will always have *his* smile *and* the praise of men, you will soon be bitterly disappointed. There will be times in your Christian walk where, if you want a close, deep relationship with God, you will be misunderstood, slandered and rejected.

Helen and I have known all these things as well as love and acceptance. God allows this to press you closer into himself, to cause you to cling to his love alone and to let go of the crutches and props of earthly praise and acknowledgement.

The Bible tells us to seek peace and pursue it; to live at peace with all men, as far as possible. But situations come from time to time which show that not everyone wishes to 'seek peace'. Satan will see to it that anything you try to do for God will not go unchallenged. He will do his best to snuff out any flame you light.

Why do we so often believe gossip and slander instead of finding out the truth? Why do we send arrows of hate and suspicion at our fellow Christians, which they may not have earned at all?

I will tell you why. We do it because *it is much easier to believe a lie than to take the trouble to find out the truth.* It is easier to point the finger accusingly than to open our arms in love.

What do you do when such things happen? Worrying and fretting do not help, anger and frustration do not help. We have had to learn to forgive, to see that these people have played into the hands of Satan and have allowed him to use them against us. We pray for them; bless them and believe that God will avenge us in his way and time; he will vindicate us and our ministry. Our 'reputation' was his business, not ours. We claim the promise of Proverbs 16,17: 'When a man's ways please the Lord, he makes even his enemies to be at peace with him.'

Sometimes people say to us: 'How wonderful it

would be to work in a firm where there are only Christians — life would be marvellous!' But these people are deluding themselves. To work with Christians is not automatically heaven on earth. It *could* be, but we are often so full of prejudice against fellow Christians, so how would we get on if we worked with them five days a week?

Some of us can't get on with Mrs Jones or Mr Turner in our own church and haven't spoken to them for years. If we worked in an office full of Christians from different denominations, there would be endless arguments on infant baptism, eternal security, the sovereignty of God or whether the Church will be going through the Tribulation, infinitum! . . . if we had no *love*.

We are sure that *our* denomination has the right doctrine and nobody understands 'the truth' quite as *we* do. We tolerate them but certainly would not go so far as treat members of 'X' church as our 'brothers and sisters in Christ'.

In many churches there are things which God does not like but if he does not hold with the *system*, he still loves the *people* in that system who are reaching out to him in the light which they have. It is *God's* business to sort them out, and *our* business to see that we walk in love and humility towards God and our brother and sister. Why do we take everything so *personally*? Jesus is the Head of the Church, not us! The Holy Spirit will guide us into *all* truth, if we are willing!

Giving mercy brings mercy to us, too. Hate does not always hurt the hated one, he may know nothing about it! But the person who is holding hatred and unforgiveness, who is feeding his resentment, is only hurting himself. Hatred and emotional turmoil release poisons into our system which will cause illness and mental torment if we do not get rid of them.

It is not always what we eat which makes us ill, but what is eating *us*. We see this clearly in Proverbs 11,17:

'The merciful man doeth good to his own soul; but he that is cruel troubleth his own flesh.' If we were God, we would probably change the system around so that the one who had hurt me should be the one to suffer. But we are not God, and he has made it that the person who will not forgive, who hates — *he* is the one who reaps a negative harvest from the seeds of bitterness he has sown.

Benjamin Franklin said: 'We judge people harshly and quickly when they make mistakes, but God will judge us at the end of our life — how we finish . . .' Yes, it is the final analysis that counts.

Helen has a quotation stuck up on the wall over her desk. It reads: 'Forgiveness is the fragrance the violet sheds on the heel that crushed it.'

Forgiveness sheds an aura of peace, fragrance and love in our lives; unforgiveness leaves an unsavoury smell, because of the rotting, hoarded-up memories we will not get rid of.

There is a Chinese proverb which says: 'A bit of fragrance always clings to the hand that gives you the roses.' If we begin to bless those who despitefully used us, the same blessing will boomerang back to us. 'Blessed are the merciful, for they shall obtain mercy,' Jesus said in Matthew 5,7 and we certainly all need that!

Stop fretting and worrying about past hurts. Give them up, forgive, receive healing for yourself.

Give someone some roses today!

25

The Curse of Condemnation

A lady came to me for counselling. Her husband had died 20 years before and although there was no real reason to do so, she blamed herself for his death. She relived every mistake, every sharp word that was said and lived under the curse of self-condemnation.

I said to her: 'We all make mistakes but God forgives us. He not only *forgives* but he *forgets*. He is not like people who often tell us — by their looks and actions, if not by words — I've forgiven you but I would just like to *remind* you that I have forgiven you, just so that we feel a twinge of guilt again! Even if you were responsible for your husband's death, which I don't believe you were, God will forgive you and wipe your slate clean. Your trouble is that you won't *forgive yourself* and are allowing the devil to keep you under condemnation. We are often harder on ourselves than God is on us.'

I prayed for her and then asked her to repeat the words: 'I forgive myself. I renounce all guilt and self-condemnation for Jesus has forgiven me. In him I am justified, in him am I cleansed, as clean today as if I had never sinned. Thank you Jesus, for delivering me now!' The depression left her face and this lady went away radiant — the load of 20 years had lifted from her.

We cannot change the past. There is not a person alive who has never made mistakes. Some people are so afraid of making a mistake that they never attempt anything worthwhile, and that is often their biggest mistake. We should learn from our mistakes and from the mistakes of others, but we must press on to new things.

The Apostle Paul must often have been reminded by the devil about his past mistakes. He had persecuted the Church, helped at Stephen's martyrdom and fought against the claims of Christ, but he realised that was all part of his old life and he had become a new person. In 2 Cor 5,17 he writes: 'If any man is in Christ he is a new creature; the old things are passed away, behold, all things are become new.' The old Saul died on the way to Damascus and a new Paul emerged who became a mighty giant for God. He forgave himself and put the past behind him.

I once knew a woman who was always reminding her husband of something he had done 18 years before. 'If only you hadn't done so-and-so, we wouldn't be in the mess we are in today.' She ranted and raved at him constantly. A wave of condemnation flooded over her husband every time he heard her and paralysed every creative thought and impulse to do better today.

What if he had made a mistake. Perhaps it was a very grave one, but she did not realise that her unforgiveness and fretting were just as bad, if not worse, in the sight of God. Proverbs 14,1 tells us: 'Every wise woman builds her house: but the foolish plucks it down with her hands.' A happy marriage and family has to be *built,* just as a house is built. Sometimes it is hard work putting one brick of love and forgiveness on top of another. This woman was literally tearing down her marriage and home with her destroying words and lack of love.

There are some things that happen which look like mistakes or defeats, but they are not. When Jesus died, it was the greatest tragedy to those who loved him. Yet he *came* to die and pay the price for our sins with his blood. He did not come just to do good works and then die a martyr's death. No, he came with the end-purpose of dying and rising again to deliver mankind. His death was *no* mistake. It was God's perfect plan. His death was a sacrifice, not a martyrdom.

Judas and Peter betrayed Jesus. Judas hanged himself; Peter became a great Apostle. What made the difference? Both saw they had done wrong. Judas saw his mistake but did not accept God's forgiveness. His guilt was so heavy that he took his own life. Peter 'wept bitterly' because he had denied the Lord in his hour of trial. He had boasted and bragged that if everyone else left Jesus, *he* would not, and that he was ready to die for him. Now he sat bowed with condemnation, a brokenhearted man. Jesus knew what Peter was feeling, but he knew that Peter had needed this experience. Peter had many great qualities but as long as he trusted in himself, he could achieve nothing worthwhile for the Kingdom of God. Jesus knew that if Peter's heart was not changed, *next time he could become a Judas!*

But Jesus never leaves us in our condemnation when we sincerely repent of our sin and mistakes, and he was getting ready to restore Peter. When the women came to the tomb and found that Jesus was risen, an angel said to them: '. . . go your way, tell his disciples *and Peter* . . .' (Mark 16,7).

Jesus sent a special message to Peter to encourage him. His words offered forgiveness and understanding, the promise of fresh communion with his Lord. It was as if he was saying: 'It doesn't matter what you have done, Peter, I *love* you. Accept my forgiveness and *forgive yourself*.' Peter came from under the curse of condemnation, a changed man.

When we are condemning ourselves for something it destroys our confidence in God. We cannot believe effectively, for a feeling of unworthiness stands like a spectre barring our path. Not long after we began the 'Voice of Renewal International' ministry, we started with radio broadcasting, one English and one German

178

programme every week. The idea was good but the timing to take on such a financial outlay was unwise. Soon we had a big bill of DM22,000 (£7,500) which we had no way of paying.

The little money which came in did not cover the expenses, let alone pay a bill like that. We stormed Heaven in prayer and praise for months but no answer came. It was hard to fight off condemnation, for the devil told us that we had brought ourselves into this mess and must get ourselves out of it. But God is more merciful than the devil and will help us out of our difficulties, even if we do go into them on our own.

One day I was in Switzerland and a pastor asked me to take a camera and some books to an English lady, who had left them there when on holiday. The next time we went to England we delivered them and the lady invited us to lunch. She was a Christian and was very interested in what we were doing in Germany. A few days later she telephoned me and said the Lord had told her to pay for us both to go to the Fountain Trust Conference in Newcastle. She had also been praying for guidance concerning some money she had inherited a short while before we came. The Lord showed her she was to give some of it towards the radio debt about which she had read in our newsletter.

This money and a further gift from Pat Robertson wiped out about two thirds of the debt. (I had been on Pat's television Christian talk show — the '700 Club' — in 1975 in Virginia Beach, USA.) The rest of the money we were able to pay off little by little. God had done a wonderful miracle for us, but it came about by throwing off condemnation and trusting him to do the impossible.

How tragic it is to see many Christians who have never realised God's great love for them. They are born-again, following Jesus, but live under a weight of condemnation, and feel constantly unworthy. In some churches many sermons are preached about humility and the necessity of being humble, but this often gets confused with 'condemnation'. A 'sin-conscious Gospel' is repeatedly brought before the eyes of the hearers.

Some of the hymns we sing speak of us as 'a worm in the dust' and 'vile sinners', and the Christian life is presented as a 'vale of tears' and a 'thorny path'. While it is true that we *were* vile sinners in God's eyes, we are now born into God's family — 'kings and priests unto God', his own children.

Further, there are tests to go through and life is not just a bed of roses, but if our Christian life is only 'a vale of tears', then we have missed some vital, Biblical truths. Some Christians are so down, they almost want to sit *under* the chair instead of *on* it, and to grovel in the dust. When you shake their hand, it feels as limp as a piece of dead fish! No life or confidence there.

In Charles Dickens' novel 'David Copperfield' there is an obnoxious character called Uriah Heep. He was the secretary of an amiable but rather weak and short-sighted gentleman, a Mr Wickfield. Uriah's main characteristic, and one which he always loved to talk about, was his extreme humility. Cracking his long, skinney fingers and looking stealthily out from red-rimmed eyes, he would fawn and bow and scrape. 'I'm so 'umble. So very 'umble.'

As the story develops, we find out that Uriah's particular brand of humility was not the genuine stuff. His 'cooking the books', blackmailing Mr Wickfield, cruelty and lying were fortunately all brought to light before he managed to take over the business and force Mr Wickfield's beautiful daughter, Agnes, to marry him, and showed the real state of his heart and thinking.

While I am not trying to say that Christians who talk a lot about humility are all like Uriah Heep, I am pointing out that there is a genuine and false humility. Genuine humility will not always be putting itself on display, but neither does it always run and hide itself. Jesus told us not to take the best seats at a party or gathering, in case you have taken somebody else's place and will have to step down, feeling very foolish. He said we should take a place which is not at the head of the table, and then if we are worthy of a better place, the host will come and escort us to our seat, and all the guests will notice and treat us with respect.

I heard the true story of a certain lady who often said: 'But I'm just a poor sinner, you know.' When a visiting preacher came, she was one of the first to buttonhole him after the service and recount a tale of her woes, ending with her usual punch line: 'But I'm just a poor sinner, you know.'

One evening, a preacher who knew her well, had just enough, and called out to the people standing around him: 'Did you know that Mrs So-and-So is a sinner? Don't you think it's time she got saved?'

There was a stunned silence, and then the lady grew red with anger and began to shout at the preacher. He just looked at her calmly, saying: 'Well, you've been telling us that for years; that's nothing new,' and walked off and left her. Her false humility had been unmasked, and pride was skulking underneath.

True humility will accept God's grace and forgiveness and rejoice in it. It is insulting to God to refuse his offer and continue to walk in our 'unworthiness'. It is *his* righteousness that we glory in, not our own. We know it is only his grace and upholding power that keeps us day by day. It is not being 'humble' to be pressed down by condemnation.

Have you ever felt uncomfortable at meeting someone because of something that has happened? This thing stands between you and you cannot feel at ease in the presence of this person. Conversation lags and you can't look him in the eye, because your heart condemns you. There is a verse in 1 John 3,21 which speaks of this, in relation to us and God:

'Beloved, if our heart condemn us not then have we confidence toward God.'

This verse reverses the situation by saying how wonderful it is to come into God's presence knowing that there is nothing between us. Every sin has been put under the blood of Jesus and we have confidence when we pray — confidence not in our own merits but because our heart does not condemn us. We can come 'boldly to the throne of grace' and receive help in time of need.

But there are situations where we feel condemned because we really have messed up our lives. We have sinned and gone our own way. We have lived according to our whims and not according to the Word of God. When we look back we realise things could have been different, and we feel worthless, sad and a failure, like the man in Robert Burns' poem:

Across the fields of yesterday
He sometimes comes to me,
A little lad just back from play –
The lad I used to be.
And yet he smiles so wistfully,
Once he has crept within,
I wonder if he hopes to see –
THE MAN I MIGHT HAVE BEEN

There are several people in the Bible whose lives could have turned out differently. There was King Saul who started out so well as King of Israel, but died on his own sword, rejected by God.

There was Gehasi, Elisha's servant. He lived day by day with this man of God, and miracles were a regular occurrence. Yet his heart was not touched. He had no longing to experience God's power in his own life, and threw his chance away. Greed and lying took over and God punished him by putting the leprosy of Naaman onto him.

182

Ananias and Sapphira in the midst of revival, with thousands of people gathering every day, thought they could lie to the Holy Spirit. Their bodies were carried out — God had struck them dead.

But for you who may be grieving over the man or woman 'you might have been', *there is a way out*. God has promised to 'restore the years that the locust has eaten'. *Physically* we cannot turn the clock back, but God has ways of restoring those years and making your latter years better than the preceding ones. If those years of sin have brought terrible consequences, pray for God's wisdom. He will show you how to come out of this situation.

Do not stay trapped in the web of condemnation. Break out today, shake off every bit of guilt that would cling to you and learn to walk in the light of God's forgiveness. Jesus does not just forgive us our past sins, but breaks the power of sin over our lives. Take this by faith. *Believe* that the curse of condemnation is broken over you and you are free to live as God intended you to be.

What does the Lord require of you? 'To do justly and to love mercy, and to walk humbly with your God' (Micah 6,8). He will give us the ability to do this!

26

A Psalm for Worriers

In the December 1964 edition of *Reader's Digest* I came across the following article:

THE '
SHEPHERD
AND THE
PSALM

By James Wallace.

Reprinted with permission from *Reader's Digest*.

Old Ferando D'Alfonso was a Basque shepherd, one of the best in his district. And rightly so, for behind him were at least 20 generations of Iberian shepherds. But D'Alfonso was more than a shepherd; he was a patriarch of his guild, the traditions and secrets of which have been handed down from generation to generation. He was full of the legends, the mysteries, the religious fervour of his native hills.

I sat with him one night under the clear, starry skies, his sheep bedded down beside a sparkling pool of water. As we were preparing to curl up in our blankets, he suddenly began a dissertation in a jargon of Greek and Basque. When he had finished, I asked him what he had said. In reply he began to quote the 23rd Psalm. There and then I learned the shepherd's literal interpretation of this beautiful poem.

'David and his ancestors,' said D'Alfonso, 'knew sheep and their ways, and David has translated a sheep's musing int simple words. The daily repetition of this Psalm fills the shepherd with reverence for his calling. Our guild takes this poem as a lodestone to guide us. It is our bulwark when the days are hot or stormy, when the nights are dark, when wild animals surround our bands. Many of its lines are statements of the simple requirements and actual duties of a Holy Land shepherd, whether he lives today or followed the same calling 6,000 years ago. Phrase by phrase, it has a well-understood meaning for us.'

The Lord is my shepherd; I shall not want

'Sheep instinctively know,' said D'Alfonso, 'that before they have been folded for the night the shepherd has planned out their grazing for the morrow. It may be that he will take them back over the same hills; it may be that he will go to a new grazing ground. They do not worry. His guidance has been good in the past, and they have faith in the future because they know he has their well-being in view.'

He maketh me to lie down in green pastures

'Sheep graze from about 3.30 in the morning until about ten. They then lie down for three or four hours and rest,' said D'Alfonso. 'When they are contentedly chewing the cud, the shepherd knows they are putting on fat. Consequently the good shepherd starts his flocks out in the early hours on the rougher herbage, moving on through the morning to the richer, sweeter grasses, and coming to a shady place for the forenoon rest in fine green pastures, best grazing of the day. Sheep resting in such happy surroundings feel contentment.'

He leadeth me beside the still waters

'Every shepherd knows,' said the Basque, 'that sheep

will not drink gurgling water. There are many small springs high in the hills of the Holy Land, whose waters run down the valleys only to evaporate in the desert sun. Although the sheep need water, they will not drink from these fast-flowing streams. The shepherd must find a place where rocks or erosion have made a little pool, or else he fashions with his hands a pocket sufficient to hold at least a bucketful.'

He restoreth my soul: He leadeth me in the paths of righteousness for His name's sake

'In the Holy Land,' went on D'Alfonso, 'each sheep takes his place in the grazing line in the morning and keeps the same position throughout the day. Once during the day, however, each sheep leaves its place and goes to the shepherd. Whereupon the shepherd stretches out his hand and rubs the animal's nose and ears, scratches its chin, whispers affectionately into its ears. The sheep, meanwhile, rubs against his leg or, if the shepherd is sitting down, nibbles at his ear and rubs its cheek against his face. After a few minutes of this communion with the master, the sheep returns to its place in the feeding line.'

Yea, though I walk through the Valley of the Shadow of Death, I will fear no evil: for Thou art with me; Thy rod and Thy staff they comfort me

'There is an actual Valley of the Shadow of Death in Palestine, and every shepherd from Spain to Dalmatia knows of it. It is south of the Jericho Road leading from Jerusalem to the Dead Sea, and it is a narrow defile through a mountain range. Climatic and grazing conditions make it necessary for the sheep to be moved through this valley for seasonal feeding each year.

'The valley is four and a half miles long. Its side walls are over 1,500 feet high in places, and it is only ten or 12 feet wide at the bottom. Travel through the valley is dangerous because its floor has gullies seven or eight feet deep. Actual footing on solid rock is so narrow in many places that a sheep cannot turn round, and it is an unwritten law of shepherds that flocks must go up the valley in the morning hours and down towards eventide, lest flocks meet in the defile.

'About half-way through the valley the walk crosses from one side to the other at a place where the path is cut in two by an eight-foot gully. One side of the gully is about 18 inches higher than the other; the sheep must jump across it. The shepherd stands at this break and coaxes or forces the sheep to make the leap. If a sheep slips and lands in the gully, the shepherd's rod is brought into play. The old-style crook circles a large sheep's neck or a small sheep's chest, and the animal is lifted to safety. If a more modern narrow crook is used, the sheep is caught about the hoofs and lifted up to the walk.

'Many wild dogs lurk in the shadows of the valley, looking for prey. The shepherd, skilled in throwing his staff, uses it as a weapon. Thus the sheep have learnt to fear no evil even in the Valley of the Shadow of Death, for their master is there to protect them from harm.'

Thou preparest a table before me in the presence of mine enemies

'David's meaning is a simple one,' said D'Alfonso, 'when conditions on the Holy Land sheep pastures are known. Poisonous plants which are fatal to grazing animals abound. Each spring the shepherd must be constantly alert. When he finds the plants, he takes his mattock and goes on ahead of the flock, grubbing out

187

every stock and root he can see. As he digs out the stocks, he lays them upon little stone pyres, some of which were built by shepherds in Old Testament days, and by the morrow they are dry enough to burn. When the pasture is free from poisonous plants, the sheep are led into it and, in the presence of their plant enemies, they eat in peace.'

Thou anointest my head with oil; my cup runneth over

'At every sheepfold there is a big earthen bowl of olive oil and a large jar of water. As the sheep come in for the night, they are led to a gate. The shepherd lays his rod across the top of the gateway just above the backs of his sheep. As each sheep passes, he quickly examines it for briers in the ears, thorns in the cheek or weeping of the eyes from dust or scratches. When such conditions are found, he drops the rod across the sheep's back and it steps out of line.

'Each sheep's wounds are carefully cleaned. Then the shepherd dips his hand into the olive oil and anoints the injury. A large cup is dipped into the jar of water, kept cool by evaporation in the unglazed pottery, and is brought out — never half full but always overflowing. The sheep will sink its nose into the water right up to the eyes, if fevered, and drink until fully refreshed.

'When all the sheep are at rest, the shepherd places his staff within reach in case it is needed during the night. Then he wraps himself in his woollen robe and lies down across the gateway, facing the sheep, for his night's repose.

'So,' concluded D'Alfonso, 'after all the care and protection the shepherd has given it, a sheep may well soliloquize in the twilight, as translated into words by David:

188

Surely goodness and mercy shall follow me all the days of my life: and I will dwell in the house of the Lord for ever.

This article gave me a better understanding of the shepherd and the sheep.

Perhaps no other Psalm has been so often quoted and so well-loved throughout the centuries as the 23rd Psalm, written by David the shepherd boy.

David who later became Israel's greatest King, from whose descendants Jesus the Messiah was born, had a humble beginning. Out on the Palestinian hillsides he watched the flock of his father's sheep, getting to know his God and learning lessons which later enabled him to rule over himself and others.

I like to read and meditate on David's Psalm like this:

THE LORD IS MY SHEPHERD. I do not need to worry. I need not worry about food for he leads me into green pastures. I need not be anxious for water because he leads me beside the still waters.

My soul can rest assured that he will restore me. Guidance in the paths of righteousness is also mine. Walking through the Valley of the Shadow of Death need not make me afraid of evil, because he is with me. His rod and staff are proof of his comfort to me.

I do not have to worry about my enemies because he prepares my table in front of their eyes. His anointing covers my head — my cup overflows.

I am sure that only good things — his goodness and his mercy — shall tenaciously follow me around as long as I live. One worry-free day I will leave this life to go and dwell with him in his glory, to enjoy his unending blessing for ever, without end.

The Lord is my very special shepherd. He is not just a

shepherd concerned about sheep, but he is concerned about me — his special sheep.

I am not just an ordinary sheep, needing only grass and water. I need such a lot more. I need clothes to wear, food to eat, shoes to walk around in. I need a place to live, a house, a room . . . I need rent money, I need transport, bus fares, a car . . . I need money for heating, I need money for my wife, clothing. I need money for my children — for shoes, meals, their education, for all of their needs.

I need money to do your work. O Lord you can see that I am quite an expensive sheep to you. I sometimes wonder if you can really afford to keep me. My worries take over the more I think on these things. My anxieties would make me feel that you cannot supply all of my needs.

When I think that you must have millions of sheep like me — some have even greater needs than mine — my small mind just gives up trying to work out how you can really do it all.

And then it slowly dawns on me that you are *not* just an ordinary shepherd. You are the *Creator, the God of the sheep: You are unlimited!*

I begin to grasp that *everything*, yes, everything in this world belongs to you. I can relax now in the knowledge that you are still in charge of my life. Just like an ordinary sheep cannot understand the shepherd, so I cannot fully understand all the ways you are leading me. The natural sheep has confidence in the shepherd, knowing that he only wants the very best for it. So I have faith in you, that you only want the very best for me.

I cast all of my worries, all of my anxieties on you, because you are wiser than I am. I accept your offer of worrying for me. I can skip around like a lamb, full of joy, because the Lord has made me so happy, that I walk as if on air. My burdens of worry have gone. I have exchanged them for *his life* — a life of FREEDOM

FROM WORRY.

Surely, the good things in life, his constant assurance that he will worry for me as long as I live, and his unending mercy — he knows my weaknesses, he knows how I want to please him by not worrying and yet so often I do *not* succeed — is new every morning. His mercy endures not only for this life but for ever.

He leads me out of *my worry* into *his care*. I can relax because he has all of my worries. He leads me along his way — the *worry-free way*.

I let my shepherd worry about all the things I cannot do. Of course, I will do my part. I will work, I will plan, I will pray — but I will deliberately leave the 'worry-part' to him; for he has worried so well for me in the past. He has worried well for the millions throughout the ages and I see no reason why he cannot do a good 'worry-job' for me.

He took *all* of my worries to the cross and *he defeated every one,* every one, every one . . . of them. *He made them his very own!* I realise that Jesus, my Shepherd, is a lot smarter than I am. I am just his sheep, he is the Creator of all things, including me.

I rejoice that he is my shepherd. I can now live a life free of worry because I have allowed my shepherd to take all of my anxieties; all of my fears, all of my worries — past and present and future — and so I am really *free* to live the way he has created me to live.

I can concentrate on living a life that is well-pleasing to him. I can use all of my energies serving him — instead of wasting them on worry!

I shall continue to live a life free from worry till one worry-free day I shall see him face to face. I know that he will welcome me home since he paid such a great price — his precious blood, his very life for me; and I shall be able to look with wonder and amazement and worship at how *he worried for me*.

I shall worship at his feet, speechless that Jesus has done such an excellent job of caring for me.

Epilogue

A student saw a sign in a bookshop-window: 'This book will save you half the work'. Thrilled, the young man ran inside and said:

'Quick, give me *two* of them!'

This book 'Winning over Worry' will not do *all* the work, *all* the learning for you, but it will be a great help to bring you out of the desert of worry into God's promised land of trust.

We have helped you to start on this worry-free road, but you must travel this path yourself. Your progress will depend on your own determination, faith and willingness to go *God's* way to finding an answer to your problems. Nobody can eat for you, you must eat for yourself. Nobody can walk this way for you, however much they want to help. There comes a point where *you* must walk it, with God's help.

The person who stands still, soon stagnates. I had a good meal last week but *today* I must eat to keep my body strong. The bread of yesterday will not satisfy today's hunger.

So do not borrow joy or sorrow from tomorrow, but live today to its fullest capacity. By overcoming worry you are making yourself available for creative living — to live life as God really intended you to live. Worry is a luxury you cannot afford!

No problem, no need will ever be greater than the power of Jesus to help you! Don't carry yesterday's or tomorrow's burdens on the shoulders of today. Live a day at a time. When you look at yourself in the mirror every morning, smile at your reflection and say:

'With the help of the Lord Jesus Christ I refuse to fret and worry about anything. I will not worry about . . . (name your problem). Worry will not pressurise and dominate me for Jesus is worrying and caring for me. And the peace of God which passes all understanding shall keep my heart and mind through Christ Jesus . . .'

Say 'Goodbye' to your worries, not 'Auf Wiedersehen' (German for 'Goodbye'). 'Auf Wiedersehen' means: I'll see you again — and you don't want that, do you?!

Go on, spoil yourself — begin to live a life free from worry!

We would be very happy to hear from you and to send you a list of our books and audio/visual publications.

Please write to:
George and Helen Jesze
Voice of Renewal UK
28 Cedar Avenue
Nuthall
Nottingham NG16 1AF
UK

or
Voice of Renewal International
P.O. Box 1145
7443 Frickenhausen
West Germany

Other Marshall Pickering Paperbacks

RICH IN FAITH

Colin Whittaker

Colin Whittaker's persuasive new book is written for ordinary people all of whom have access to faith, a source of pure gold even when miracles and healing seem to happen to other people only.

The author identifies ten specific ways to keep going on the road to faith-riches, starting where faith must always begin—with God himself, the Holy Spirit, the Bible, signs and wonders, evangelism, tongues and finally to eternal life with Christ.

OUR GOD IS GOOD

Yonggi Cho

This new book from Pastor Cho describes the blessings, spiritual and material, that reward the believer. Yonggi Cho presents his understanding of the fullness of salvation, bringing wholeness to God's people.

HEARTS AFLAME
Stories from the Church of Chile

Barbara Bazley

Hearts Aflame is a book suffused with love for the large, sometimes violent country of Chile and joy at the power of the Gospel taking root.

Each chapter is a story in itself, telling of some encounter, episode of friendship that has left its mark on the author's life.

THE PLIGHT OF MAN AND THE POWER OF GOD

Dr Martin Lloyd-Jones

The text of one of the highly esteemed sermons given by Dr Martin Lloyd-Jones, based on verses from Romans, Chapter One, focuses on our need to be entirely committed to the Christian gospel.

Dr Lloyd-Jones highlights the uniqueness of the faith. Because of this he stresses the necessity of our absolute commitment to Christ and his call to us.

This book will be of great interest to all thoughtful Christians and of help to preachers, speakers and students.

THE NATURAL TOUCH

Kim Swithinbank

Some people think of 'evangelism' as knocking on doors, reading your Bible on the train or starting up conversations with strangers in which you get on to the four-point-plan of salvation as quickly as possible. Some of these activities we would do, others we'd cringe at doing.

In his first book, Kim Swithinbank says that sharing our hope in Christ is something that we are *all* asked to do. It should be as natural as breathing to us.

Taking us through the most common obstacles which keep people away from Christianity, he shows how we can develop a lifestyle which is attractive and compelling for Christ.

Kim Swithinbank is Director of Evangelism at All Souls, Langham Place.

THE NEW KESWICK COLLECTION

'Messages given at Keswick have brought spiritual enlightenment, refreshment and challenge to God's people all over the world, so I welcome the launch of *The New Keswick Collection*.'
JOHN STOTT

'God meets with many people and they with Him at Keswick year by year. I am delighted that the great themes of the Convention are now being more fully put down into print that many others may also meet with God and He with them.'
MICHAEL A. BAUGHEN, BISHOP OF CHESTER

'I warmly commend this new series.'
ERIC J. ALEXANDER

In the first volume, *What He Says, Where He Sends*, Philip Hacking deals with the subject of mission, and challenges all Christians to a life of more committed service.

THE TORN VEIL

Esther Gulshan with Thelma Sangster

Gulshan Fatima, the youngest daughter of a Muslim family, lived a quietly secluded life at home in the Punjab. A trip to England began a spiritual awakening that led ultimately to her conversion to Christianity. She has since preached to thousands of Muslims and many have not only found faith but have, like her, found physical healing.

If you wish to receive *regular information* about *new books*, please send your name and address to:

London Bible Warehouse
PO Box 123
Basingstoke
Hants RG23 7NL

Name...

Address ....

....

....

....

I am especially interested in:

☐ Biographies
☐ Fiction
☐ Christian living
☐ Issue related books
☐ Academic books
☐ Bible study aids
☐ Children's books
☐ Music
☐ Other subjects